每天读一点英文

Everyday English Snack

那些光影飞华的魅惑

The shinning and popular words

章华◎编译

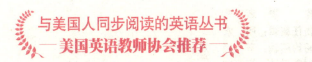

与美国人同步阅读的英语丛书
——美国英语教师协会推荐——

陕西师范大学出版社

图书在版编目（CIP）数据

那些光影飞华的魅惑：英汉对照/章华编译. —西安：
陕西师范大学出版社,2009.8
（每天读一点英文）
ISBN 978-7-5613-4789-8

Ⅰ. 那… Ⅱ. 章… Ⅲ. ①英语—汉语—对照读物
②散文—作品集—世界 Ⅳ. H319.4：I

中国版本图书馆 CIP 数据核字（2009）第 146809 号

图书代号：SK9N0802

上架建议：英语学习

那些光影飞华的魅惑（时尚卷）

作　　者：章　华
责任编辑：周　宏
特约编辑：辛　艳　刘宇圣
封面设计：张丽娜
版式设计：风　筝
出版发行：陕西师范大学出版社
　　　　　　（西安市陕西师大 120 信箱　邮编：710062）
印　　刷：北京嘉业印刷厂
开　　本：880×1230　1/32
字　　数：210 千字
印　　张：7.5
版　　次：2009 年 9 月第一版
印　　次：2012 年 1 月第四次印刷
ISBN 978-7-5613-4789-8
定　　价：21.80 元

目 录
CONTENTS

我的美丽日记
My beautiful diary

我的健康我做主
My health, my way

时尚达人
Look to those fashion icons

勇闯天涯
Globe trekker

摩登时代
Modern times

The shinning and popular words

那些光影飞华的魅惑

我的美丽日记
My beautiful diary

The Misunderstandings on Beauty

你陷入美容护肤误区了吗?

1.Soap is Bad for Your Skin

Traditionally, *soap was a mix of animal fats and fruit or vegetable oils*. This **combination** has a high PH and is drying to skin, particularly to aging skin. These days, however, soaps are formulated with synthetic elements that are milder than traditional soap, and therefore suitable to cleanse skin. Most soaps have emollients (moisturisers) added, so they are **beneficial** for the skin. If you prefer the cleansing feeling which soap provides, don't let those purveyors of fine skincare bully you—there's nothing wrong with using soap.

2.Dry Skin Causes Wrinkles

Around eighty percent of lines and wrinkles are caused by the sun. The other twenty percent are the result of facial expressions such as smiling and frowning. If you smoke, the appearance of these wrinkles is accelerated. Also, as one ages the skin makes less natural oil and this makes the wrinkling more apparent. A moisturiser will help temporarily smooth away some early fine lines. Protect yourself from the sun, and you impede the development of fine lines. Remember, a tan is your skin's reaction to an injury.

3.It Can Be Too Late to Start Wearing Sunscreen

The cumulative effect of the sun's rays causes a multitude of damage to skin, but it's never too late to start protecting skin from the sun. There is clinical evidence that once you start protecting the skin, it has the ability to repair itself. This repair is not going to happen overnight ;it's a gradual process that can take a couple years to yield significant results. Do your skin a favour and start the day with a layer of sunscreen. And remember to wear sunscreen during the winter. Just because you don't feel the sun's rays, doesn't mean its harmful UVA and UVB rays are not **penetrating** your skin. If you can see shadows, you need to protect your skin.

4.Everyone needs Moisturiser

According to dermatologists, you only need a moisturiser if your skin experiences the following: redness, scaliness or itchiness. These symptoms are more **frequently** seen during the colder seasons.

5.For Best Results You Should Stick to One Product Line

You may love how all the products work together, but using products from different lines won't kill you. Every cosmetics line has products you should avoid because they contain **irritating** ingredients, inadequate amounts of sunscreen, or moisturisers that over-saturate the skin. Experiment and find the products that are right for you.

6.Expensive Products are Better

Completely untrue. All cosmetics contain standard cosmetic ingredients. They can't contain anything else, as drugs do, or they would be regulated differently. The quality levels of cosmetic ingredients don't vary that much, and every company that buys cosmetic-grade ingredients all buy the same quality.

7.Eating Chocolate and Fried Foods Causes Bad Skin

Studies have shown that pimples are caused from factors such as extreme stress or dead skin cells blocking pores. However, eating fresh fruits and raw vegetables does promote a healthier complexion due to their vitamins and minerals.

8.Frequent Trimmings Can Make Hair Grow Faster

Hair, whether it is cut or not, grows about half an inch per month. Hair does grow slightly faster in the summer, but that is due to hormones rather than the stylist's scissors. A worrying trend among young Chinese girls is to rub a paste made of crushed contraceptive pill into their scalp and hair. This does not lead to stronger, glossier, faster growing hair. In fact, the hormones, while **initially** improving the condition of the hair, quickly lead to hair loss.

P.S. You can't repair split ends. The only way to rid of split ends is to cut them off and prevent them in the future with good hair care. A good trim will eliminate split ends, making hair look healthier and livelier.

9.Shaving Makes Hair Grow Back Darker and Coarser

As above. Cutting or shaving any hair on your body does not affect it growth.

10.You Can Get Rid of Cellulite

The truth is, nothing can be done to permanently eliminate cellulite—not even liposuction. *The removal of cellulite remains one of the holy grails of cosmetic dermatology.* It doesn't matter whether you're fat or thin, rich or poor, luck of the gene pool determines who will and won't get cellulite. Take heart though, you can, however, **temporarily** reduce its orange peel-like appearance. Specialist firming creams containing caffeine tighten and smooth the skin, while basic moisturisers will also work to hydrate and swell the skin, making cellulite a little less obvious.

1. 香皂对皮肤有害

从传统上来说，香皂是动物脂肪和水果或植物油的混合体。这种化合物的 PH 值很高，会令皮肤，尤其是老化的皮肤，变得干燥。现如今的香皂在配方中加入了较传统香皂更为温和的人工合成成分，因而适合清洁皮肤。大多数香皂都添加了润肤剂(润肤霜)，所以对肌肤有益。如果你更喜欢用香皂洁肤的那种感觉，那么就别让那些高档护肤品的经销商们把你给唬住了——使用香皂一点儿问题都没有。

2. 干燥皮肤造成皱纹

约80%的细纹和皱纹是由阳光造成的。另外的20%则源于微笑和皱眉等面部表情。如果你吸烟,皱纹就长得更快。另外,随着一个人年龄的增长,皮肤分泌的天然油脂会减少,而这会令皱纹更加明显。润肤霜能暂时抚平一些早期的细纹。避免让自己受到日晒,你就能抑制细纹的发展。记住:晒黑就是你皮肤受损的反应。

3. 想要开始涂防晒霜时可能为时已晚

日积月累的日晒会对皮肤造成严重损害,但是什么时候开始让皮肤避免日晒都不晚。临床证明,一旦你开始保护你的皮肤,它就拥有了自我修复的能力。这种修复不会在一夜之间发生;它是一个循序渐进的过程,可能需要几年的时间才会产生显著的效果。帮帮你的皮肤吧,涂上一层防晒霜再开始一天的生活。此外,在冬天也要记得涂防晒霜。你感觉不到阳光,并不意味着紫外线A和紫外线B不会伤害到你的皮肤。只要能看到影子,就需要保护你的皮肤。

4. 人人都需要润肤霜

根据皮肤科医生的说法,只有在你的肌肤出现以下状况时你才需涂润肤霜:发红、多鳞或发痒。这些症状在天气寒冷时更为常见。

5. 为了达到最佳效果,你应该坚持使用同一系列的产品

你可能喜欢整套产品一起使用的效果,但使用不同系列的

产品也不会对你有所伤害。每个化妆品系列都有你该避免使用的产品，因为它们含有刺激性成分、含量不足的防晒成分或是过度滋润肌肤的润肤剂。要在试用后找出适合自己的产品。

6. 产品越贵越好

完全不属实。所有化妆品都含有化妆品所需的标准成分。它们不会像药品一样含有其他物质，否则它们会受到不同的管制。化妆品成分的质量等级相差不是很大，每家化妆品公司所购原料的质量都是相同的。

7. 吃巧克力和油炸食品对皮肤不好

研究表明，粉刺是由过度压力或死皮细胞阻塞毛孔等因素所致。然而，多吃富含维生素和矿物质的新鲜水果和蔬菜确实对皮肤有好处。

8. 经常修发会使其长得更快

无论剪发与否，头发都会以每月约半英寸的速度生长。头发在夏季的确会长得稍快一些，但那要归功于荷尔蒙而非发型师的剪刀。在中国的年轻女性中出现了一股令人担忧的风尚，那就是将避孕药碾成粉末弄成糊，涂到头皮和头发上。这不会使头发更加坚韧、更有光泽、长得更快。事实上，荷尔蒙虽然在最初会改善发质，但转而就会导致脱发。

此外，你不可能修复分叉。摆脱分叉的唯一方法就是将其剪掉并精心护理头发以防其日后再现。修剪得好就会清除分叉，令头发看上去更加健康和洒脱。

9. 剃除毛发会令其长得更黑更粗糙

如上所述，修剪或剃除身上的任何毛发都不会影响其生长。

10. 你可以摆脱脂肪团

事实上，做什么都无法永久去除脂肪团——甚至吸脂也不行。去除脂肪团至今仍是皮肤美容学上的终极目标之一。它与你的胖瘦、贫富无关，基因库的随机性决定了谁会拥有或没有脂肪团。尽管如此，还是要振作起来，你可以暂时缓解皮肤呈橘皮状的现象。含有咖啡因的专业紧肤霜会紧致和平滑肌肤，而一般的润肤霜有补水的功效，这能使脂肪团看起来不那么明显。

❦单词注解❦

combination [ˌkɔmbiˈneiʃən] *n.* 结合（体）；联合（体）

beneficial [beniˈfiʃəl] *adj.* 有益的；有利的

penetrate [ˈpenitreit] *v.* 穿过；刺入；透过

frequently [ˈfriːkwəntli] *adv.* 频繁地，屡次地

irritate [ˈiriteit] *v.* 使恼怒；使烦躁

initially [iˈniʃəli] *adv.* 最初；开头

temporarily [ˈtempərerili] *adv.* 暂时地；临时地

❦实用句型 & 词组❦

The plants should be protected from the cold.（保护）

He can't get rid of the cold.（摆脱）

Her absence was due to the storm.（因为，由于）

❦翻译行不行❦

从传统上来说，香皂是动物脂肪和水果或植物油的混合体。

_____

研究表明，粉刺是由过度压力或死皮细胞阻塞毛孔等因素所致。

_____

去除脂肪团至今仍是皮肤美容学上的终极目标之一。

_____

Using the Force of Yoga

接触瑜伽的神奇力量

As our knowledge of health and fitness increases, people are becoming more and more interested in not only taking care of themselves physically, but mentally and spiritually as well. As a result, many are turning to more complete approaches to health, including less **mainstream** fitness methods such as yoga.

Yoga's **origins** lie in Hindu philosophy, which was developed thousands of years ago in India. Today, yoga is a system of movements and meditation that emphasizes physical control and discipline as a way to achieve a state of spiritual knowledge.

Yoga's ideal state of knowledge is reached after a person has gone through eight different stages. These include aspects of self-control, religion, **postures**, regulation of breath, restraint of senses, steadying of the mind, meditation, and profound thought. *For a practitioner of yoga, or "yogi" the progression through these stages is a movement from the physical toward a perfect mental state.*

*There are eight major schools of yoga, each **varying** in its area of emphasis.* The type of yoga that is taught in the West is mainly a combination of exercise and meditation called Hatha Yoga. Hatha Yoga is said to have a number of positive effects, such as reducing weight, strengthening muscles and nerves, cleaning out the body, and generally improving health and prolonging life.

Recent decades have seen yoga gain widespread acceptance as a method of staying in shape, as well as a way of handling stress. Pop singer Madonna and super model Christy Turlington are just two of the many celebrities known to be strong advocates of yoga.

At present, there is a lot of speculation and uncertainty about yoga and its **effects**. *One thing, however, is certain: In our modern world of fast-paced lifestyles, taking time out to meditate and do some relaxing exercise cannot be a bad thing!*

随着我们对健康与健身的知识与日俱增，人们在关心身体健康的同时，越来越关注心理与精神的健康。因此，许多人转而寻求更全面的途径来增进健康，包括一些还未成为主流的健身方式，如瑜伽。

瑜伽起源于印度哲学，这种哲学在印度已经发展了数千年。如今，瑜伽是一组强调身体控制与修身养性的运动和静坐，是达到"天人合一"这种境界的一个有效途径。

一般要经过 8 个不同阶段的训练才能达到瑜伽的完美境界。这包括了自制、信仰、体位、调息、节欲、内省、冥想和三摩地。对瑜伽修习者来说，这些阶段是从身体到完美精神境界的进程。

瑜伽有 8 大流派，每派强调的领域各有不同。西方国家传授的瑜伽名为"哈他瑜伽"（又称"运动瑜伽"），主要是运动与静坐的结合。据说"哈他瑜伽"有许多良效，如减肥、强化肌肉与神经、净化身体进而增进健康，延年益寿。

近几十年来，瑜伽已广为世人接受，成为一种既能保持身材又能舒缓压力的方法。有许多知名人士极力推荐瑜伽，流行歌手麦当娜与超级名模克里斯蒂·特灵顿就是其中两位。

目前，关于瑜伽及其作用有很多揣测与怀疑。然而，有一点是毋庸置疑的：在快节奏的现代生活中，花点时间静坐和做些放松身体的运动，绝不是件坏事！

❧单词注解❧

mainstream ['meinstriːm] *n.* 主流

origin ['ɔridʒin] *n.* 起源；由来

posture ['pɔstʃə] *n.* 姿势，姿态

vary ['vεəri] *v.* 使不同；变更；修改

widespread ['waidspred] *adj.* 普遍的；广泛的

effect [i'fekt] *n.* 效果，效力；作用

❧实用句型 & 词组❧

Please take care of the baby for me for a while, will you?（照顾）

A number of people have left.（一些）

He speaks Spanish as well as English.（和……一样好）

❧翻译行不行❧

对瑜珈修习者来说，这些阶段是从身体到完美精神境界的进程。

_____

一般要经过 8 个不同阶段的训练才能达到瑜伽的完美境界。

_____

有件事是毋庸置疑的：在快节奏的现代生活中，花点时间静坐和做些放松身体的运动，绝不是件坏事！

_____

Is Higher SPF better?

不畏强光，智慧防晒

There are many **misconceptions** with sunscreen. *You have those people who think that getting the highest SPF will protect them better than a lower SPF.* Then, there are those who won't use sunscreen with a high SPF because they think they won't get a **tan**.

Here are the facts.

Higher SPF's aren't always necessary. You need to look at a couple of things when you are shopping for sunscreen. First, how light is your skin tone? *Those with lighter skin will usually burn faster than those with darker or olive skin.* If your skin starts to turn red fast, you'll want a higher SPF.

But what does the SPF rating really mean?

SPF stands for Sun Protection Factor. To figure out how long you are safe from the sun (at least the UVB rays) you need to do a little math. Take the number of SPF and **multiply** it by 10. That is the time that if you were under perfect conditions, you'd be safe from the sun's rays.

For example: SPF 20 x 10 = 200 minutes of sun protection.

Perfect conditions mean that you aren't in water or sweating. *Because you want to be safe from the sun, I'd **recommend** applying every 1–2 hours, no matter the SPF.*

对于防晒，有不少误区。很多人认为高 SPF 比低 SPF 防晒的效果更好。还有一些人认为自己不会晒黑，所以根本不需要高防晒指数的防晒霜。

然而事实并非如此。

高的防晒指数并非总是必需的。当你购买防晒霜时，你需要考虑以下几点。首先，你的肤色如何？亮色皮肤的人较暗色或橄榄色肌肤的人更容易晒伤。如果你的肌肤很容易变红，那你就需要高防晒指数的防晒霜。

但是防晒指数等级到底指的是什么呢？

SPF 是防晒系数的意思。需要计算一下才能知道你在太阳下可以待多久而不会被晒伤（至少不被 UVB 射线晒伤）。将 SPF 系数乘以 10 得出来的时间就是防晒产品的保护时间。

例如：SPF20 的防晒产品可以保护 200 分钟之久。

理想的条件意味着你不是在水里或是在出汗。要做到防晒，我的建议是，不管防晒系数是多少，每隔一两个小时涂一次防晒霜。

🌿单词注解🌿

misconception ['miskən'sepʃən] *n.* 误解；错误想法

tan [tæn] *v.* 硝（皮）；使晒成棕褐色

multiply ['mʌltipli] *v.* 乘；使繁殖

recommend [rekə'mend] *v.* 推荐，介绍

🌿实用句型 & 词组🌿

I can't figure him out.（理解）

He wants you to see him in London without fail.（要，想要）

No matter what happened, he would not mind.（不管）

🌿翻译行不行🌿

很多人认为高 SPF 比低 SPF 防晒的效果更好。

_____

亮色皮肤的人较暗色或橄榄色肌肤的人更容易晒伤。

_____

要做到防晒，我的建议是，不管防晒系数是多少，每隔一两个小时涂一次防晒霜。

_____

The Guide to What University Girls Are Wearing

校园 MM，穿衣有道

What kinds of clothes do college girls need for school? When thinking about what to buy and what to bring, here's one word to keep in mind: **practical**! You can be a campus fashion icon if that makes you happy, but most students prefer to spend their time and money on other things. *College life is stressful, and you're going to want to be comfortable more often than you'll want to be stylish.*

So what kinds of clothes should you bring to college? Here are a few practical fashion tips.

Bring comfortable clothes

You may be the type who doesn't mind a little discomfort in the name of fashion, and that's fine. But there will be days when **cozy** clothes are a must, like during finals or the day after a nasty breakup, so make sure you have them on hand. Think T-shirts, sweats, and cozy jeans.

Wear comfortable walking shoes

Unless you enjoy being miserable, this is mandatory. Ladies, please don't walk around **campus** in high-heeled pumps. This isn't *Sex and the City*—it's a college campus, and you're going to be walking constantly. Save the cute heels for the weekend.

Bring low maintenance clothes

Time is at a **premium** in college. If it needs hand washing, don't bring it. Heck, if it needs ironing, don't bring it.

Bring weather appropriate clothes

Keep in mind that you'll be walking around campus all the time, so if your school is in a cold climate, bring a heavy coat, scarf, gloves, and **waterproof** boots. Wear whatever you need to keep warm even if it messes up your outfit. *If whomever it is you're trying to impress likes you less with hat hair, this isn't someone worthy of your attention.*

Don't come to class half naked

Save the sexy stuff for the weekends, and come to class looking a little more professional. *If you wear a micro-mini skirt, pair it with a big sweater.*

Bring clothes you can layer

You're going to be coming in from the cold into overheated classrooms, and in from the heat into classrooms fit for a **polar** bear.

　　大学女生应该穿什么样的衣服呢？当你想自己应该买什么和带什么的时候，有一个原则要时刻牢记：实用！当然如果成为大学时尚达人让你觉得很幸福，你也可以朝这个方向努力。不过大多数的学生还是喜欢把自己的时间和金钱花在别的事情上。大学生活压力重重，在舒适与时尚之间，大家总会偏向前者。

　　那大学生应该穿什么样的衣服呢？下面是一些实用的流行小贴士：

穿舒适的衣服

　　也许你可以忍受为了时尚而牺牲一下自己的舒适度，这无可厚非。但总有一天，比如在期末考试期间或者在和男朋友分手后，你会发现自己迫切需要舒适的衣服，所以务必在衣橱里备几件舒适的服装。你可以考虑 T 恤、毛衣和修身牛仔裤等。

穿轻便的鞋子

　　如果你不想遭罪的话，这可是一件必需品。女孩子们，请千万不要穿着高跟鞋在大学校园里走来走去。这里不是《欲望都市》——这里是大学校园，你是要在这里不停走动的。把高跟鞋留到周末穿吧。

穿容易保养的衣服

在大学生活中，时间就是一切。那些需要手洗和熨烫的衣物，通通不要穿。

穿适合时节的衣服

请你记住，你会经常在校园里走动，所以如果学校很冷的话，一定要穿厚实的外套、围巾、手套和防水靴。尽量穿保暖的衣物，即便这会使你的形象打点折扣。如果你心仪的那个人喜欢你穿的少一点，那么这个人绝对不值得你为之付出。

不要穿暴露的衣服去上课

性感的衣服还是留在周末穿吧，上课还是穿得比较正式点好。如果穿迷你裙，就搭件宽松的毛衣吧。

备些易于穿脱的衣服

你需要从寒冷的校园步入温暖的教室，也需要从温暖的室内切换到寒冷的户外。

单词注释

practical ['præktikəl] *adj.* 实践的，实际的

cozy ['kəuzi] *adj.* 舒适的；惬意的

campus ['kæmpəs] *n.* 校园，校区

premium ['primjəm] *n.* 额外补贴，津贴；酬金

waterproof ['wɔ:təpru:f] *adj.* 不透水的，防水的

polar ['pəulə] *adj.* 北极的，南极的；极地的

funky ['fʌnki] *adj.* 惊恐的；畏缩的

实用句型 & 词组

At the moment, he preferred not to think about the future. (宁愿)

He is aimless to walk around. (到处走动)

She picked up a dress appropriate for the occasion. (适当的)

翻译行不行

大学生活压力重重，在舒适与时尚之间，大家总会偏向前者。

_____

如果你心仪的那个人喜欢你穿的少一点，那么这个人绝对不值得你为之付出。

_____

如果穿迷你裙，就搭件宽松的毛衣吧。

_____

Tips to Improve Your Figure

塑身小秘方，让瘦身更有趣

In a perfect world, the only thing that you would need to do to reach your fitness goals would be work out occasionally. Unfortunately, the only way to truly get the body and level of health that you want is through the **combination** of diet and exercise.

If there is anything I have learned through my years as a personal trainer is that dieting right is the number one obstacle people face while trying to get fit. But filling your plate with healthy food doesn't have to be a **miserable** experience.

Here are the best strategies I have found to keep people in shape.

Give Yourself Some Flexibility — If you box yourself into too strict of a diet, you are setting yourself up for failure. It's true that for most people if you want to lose weight, it is going to have to involve cutting back a bit on how much you eat, but if you allow yourself nothing but rice cakes and unbuttered wheat toast, you turn yourself into a ticking time bomb that will go off onto the nearest piece of cheesecake. Expect that you are going to **indulge** a little every now and then, and accept it.

Make Your Foods Easy to Make—I've discovered that most people eat junk food because it's just so darn convenient. Microwaveable pizzas take three minutes to make, and there is a fast food joint on every corner who can give you a greasy pre heated burger in a matter of seconds. The only real way to **counteract** this is by making your healthy food just as convenient as unhealthy food.

For example, you might keep some whole grain tortillas in your cupboard so that you can make a quick and easy burrito with lean chicken or beans. You might also keep some frozen vegetables in your freezer, because they can be heated fairly quickly and be ready to eat. You may also consider buying lots of canned soups, because they take little time to prepare and are often very low in calories.

Find Ways to Combat Stress — Whenever someone has a relapse in their diet, it is usually during a particularly **stressful** time in their life. Maybe dealing with a toddler has kept them awake for much of a few nights or their new job is giving them a lot to worry about. This is when people start binging on French fries and ice cream. But if you want to conserve your waistline, you need to find other ways to combat stress.

The best way to deal with this by recognizing times when you might be getting stressed and react too it. If you find the pressure building up, find some time for yourself to do something that you really enjoy. Just half an hour of "me time" can make your diet go along a lot more smoothly.

Cut Out the Liquid Calories — If it has calories and comes in a liquid form, try to limit your intake of it. The reason is that stuff like soda, alcohol, and milk can add a bunch of calories to your daily diet, but they never make you feel full. So you feel hungry even as you consume far more calories than you need. Focus mostly on whole foods and use tea or water to **satisfy** your thirst.

Fitness Expert Chris McCombs is a Personal Trainer in Hollywood California. *While walking out of a burrito joint Chris discovered a radical approach to burning fat at a rapid rate which he helps people all over do today.* Chris is also a personal training marketing expert and helps personal trainers and other people in the fitness industry to triple their income and cut their work hours by more than half.

在这样的一个美好的世界里，你所需要做的一件事情就是怎样有条理的达到你的塑身目标。然而，不幸的是，为了能够真正达到你所想要的体魄和健康的标准，唯一的办法就是节食加锻炼。

如果问我作为一个私人教练这么多年学到了什么的话，那就是：正确的节食是每个希望拥有好身材的人所面临的最大问题。实际上，健康的饮食并不是什么痛苦的经历。

以下就是我发现的适合人们保持好身材的最佳策略。

给自己一个适应的时间——如果你太克制节食的话，那注定是要失败的。的确，对大多数人来讲，为了减轻体重，就必须在原先饮食的量上有所削减。但如果除了年糕及没有奶油的烤面包你什么都不吃的话，现在的你就是颗定时炸弹，在不经意的一块酪饼后，体重就会突然暴增，所有计划都会付诸东流。除非在你能接受的范围内，不时地让自己享受一下。

学会制作简单的食品——我发现许多人喜欢吃剩菜剩饭，因为这很方便。把比萨放进微波炉里，三分钟就可以吃了。而且，在我们周围的每个角落都会有快餐店为你服务——提供一个有油脂并热气腾腾的汉堡牛肉饼只是几秒钟的事情。与之抗衡的唯一方法就是，让自己制作的食品如同快餐食品那么方便。

比如说，在你的橱柜里可能会存有谷粒的玉米粉薄烙饼，你可以用这些材料做成一个由纯鸡肉或土豆泥做馅的面饼卷。你也可以在你的冰箱里储存一些冷冻的蔬菜，因为它们容易解冻，方便食用。你也可以考虑买一些罐装的汤，因为这些不用花太多的时间去准备，而且所含的卡路里也不多。

找到抗压力的方法——一旦某人在他的节食计划中出现了旧病复发的状态，那么这个阶段一般是他在生活中压力最大的时段。可能为了照顾小孩，他们很多个夜晚不能好好的入睡，也有可能是他们的新工作并不能让他们安心。于是他们便开始钟情于法国炸薯条和冰淇淋。然而，如果你想保持你的身材的话，你必须找到其他的抗压力方法。

最好的办法就是，你首先要清楚自己在什么时候压力最大。一旦你感受到了压力，你应该给自己一点时间做自己真正喜欢的事情。即使只是短短的"自我半小时"，都能让你的节食计划顺利地进行。

拒绝液体卡路里——尽量限制以液体的形式吸收卡路里。因为，像汽水，酒精及牛奶这样的饮品就会在你的日常饮食中增加热量，但你永远都不会有饱的感觉。即使你吸收的热量已经超过了你的所需，但你仍有饿的感觉。所以，要尽量食用有机食品，茶或水是解渴的首选。

瘦身专家克里斯•麦克白是美国加州好莱坞的一个私人教练。他发现了一个快速燃烧脂肪的方法，他现在就是利用这个方法来帮助人们减肥。克里斯在私人训练市场方面也是个专家，他不仅是私人教练，也为健身锻炼行业的其他从业者提供帮助，让他们在减少一半的工作时间里增加三倍的收入。

健身小贴士

1. 锻炼前要检查身体，注意过去所患的疾病及运动损伤、药物服用的情况，患有传染性疾病的人不可进行水中锻炼。

2. 孕妇、发烧或体温过低者及有运动损伤，如崴脚、拉伤者不宜参加水中锻炼。运动前后需要各做 5 分钟的准备活动，让肌肉先预热一下，然后再下水。

❧单词注释❧

combination [ˌkɔmbiˈneiʃən] *n.* 结合（体）；联合（体）

miserable [ˈmizərəbl] *adj.* 痛苦的；不幸的

indulge [inˈdʌldʒ] *v.* 沉迷于；满足

counteract [ˌkauntəˈrækt] *v.* 对……起反作用；对抗；抵消

stressful [ˈstresfəl] *adj.* 紧张的；压力重的

satisfy [ˈsætisfai] *v.* 使满意，使高兴

❧实用句型 & 词组❧

The boy is still too young to go to school. (太……以致不能……)

He had so many falls that he was black and blue all over. （以便）

He has learnt to deal properly with all kinds of complicated situations.

（处理）

❧翻译行不行❧

在这样的一个美好的世界里，你所需要做的一件事情就是怎样有条理的
达到你的塑身目标。

_____

最好的办法就是，你首先要清楚自己在什么时候压力最大。

_____

他发现了一个快速燃烧脂肪的方法，他现在就是利用这个方法来帮助人
们减肥。

_____

The Guide to Colour-Matching
白领着装色彩指南

You are what you wear! Keeping your clothes well-pressed will keep you from looking hard-pressed.

Colors and their **signals**

Black suggests authority and seriousness. It is a dignified choice that announces your presence, but can be intimidating if overused.

*Pastels are soothing colors, and promote friendliness while discouraging **aggression**.*

White symbolizes purity, cleanliness, and sophistication. It works well as a shirt. Women can pull it off as a suit, but men steer clear!

Grey offers you a **dignified** and conservative authority. If it's too light, you could seem passive or weak.

Navy Blue clothing demands respect. *It also conveys a feeling of loyalty, integrity, and dependability.*

Brown symbolizes reliability, and tends to make people feel comfortable. However, it can suggest a lack of **authority**.

着装是你的名片！衣服穿得精神，人才显得从容。

颜色及其传递的信号

黑色象征权威与肃穆。选择它，威严而富有地位，但如果运用过度，则可能令人生畏。

彩色是柔和的颜色，有助于增进友谊，减少攻击性。

白色象征纯洁、洁净和成熟。一件白衬衫的效果非常不错。女性可以选其作为套装的颜色，而男性则不要选择白色套装！

灰色让你显得威严、庄重、权威。如果是很淡的灰色，则可能让你看上去被动而软弱。

深蓝色服装容易赢得尊重。这种颜色同时也传达出忠实、诚信和可靠的讯息。

褐色象征可靠，给人一种舒适的感觉。然而，它同时也意味着缺乏权威性。

单词注释

signal ['signl] *n.* 信号；暗号

aggression [ə'greʃən] *n.* 侵略；侵略行动

dignify ['dignifai] *v.* 使有尊严，使高贵

authority [ɔː'θɔriti] *n.* 权，权力；职权

实用句型 & 词组

He pulled off his overcoat and began to work. （脱下）

Modern furniture design tends to simplicity. （有……的倾向）

Lack of interest is a guarantee of failure. （缺少）

翻译行不行

着装是你的名片！衣服穿得精神，人才显得从容。

_____

彩色是柔和的颜色，有助于增进友谊，减少攻击性。

_____

这种颜色同时也传达出忠实、诚信和可靠的讯息。

_____

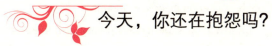 今天，你还在抱怨吗？

"Any fool can criticize, condemn, and **complain** but it takes character and self control to be understanding and forgiving." —Dale Carnegie

If we really want to be happy, why do we act like such babies?

We can claim to be proactive in our life by settings goals and going after what we want. But if we're always whining and complaining, are we really living **effectively**?

If you don't believe me, count how many times you complain about something or other in one day. Whether it be being stuck in traffic, being bothered by the weather, not enough mustard on your sandwich, or whatever it is, there are endless instances where you can find a reason to complain.

But it's not just outside circumstances that we complain about. We complain about ourselves too. We complain that we don't have enough time, we don't have enough money (this one is huge because it's often "true"), that we're not smart enough, cool enough, or just enough.

I know I've experienced plenty of unpleasantness **due** to complaining about things I can't control. I never really thought about it much until I found this website about "living in a complain free world."

Imagine how much happier you would be if you simply stopped complaining? Much of what you complain about is outside of your control anyway. What's the point of brooding about something you have no power to change? Not very intelligent, if you ask me.

Simply becoming **conscious** of how much you complain is the first step to stopping. When you recognize that you're complaining, stop and take notice of it. Ask yourself if you would rather complain, or be happy.

Are you ready to live a complaint-free, happier life?

任何笨蛋都可以批评，谴责和抱怨，但是理解和宽容需要个人品质和自我控制。

——卡内基

如果我们想要变得高兴，为什么要像小孩子那样呢？

我们可以积极主动的在我们生活中设定目标，然后向着目标进发。但是如果我们整天牢骚满腹，怨天尤人的话，我们还会活的有效率吗?

如果你不相信我,仔细想想你一天要抱怨几次。不管是因为糟糕的交通状况,被天气所困扰,还是三明治上芥末放得不够,总之生活中有无数的烦心事可以让我们抱怨。

不仅外部的环境让我们抱怨,我们还不断的抱怨我们自己。比如时间不够啊,钱不够花啊,不够聪明不够冷静啊,反正什么看上去都不够好。

很多时候,不愉快都是因为抱怨自己不能控制的事情。我没有仔细的思考过这个问题,直到有一天我发现一个叫"活在没有抱怨的世界中"的网站。

想想吧,如果你停止抱怨的话,你会变得多么的快乐。反正那些事情又无力改变,整天想着那些你无力改变的事情有什么意义呢?如果你来问我,我会说那样很愚蠢。

停止抱怨要做的第一步就是想清楚你在抱怨什么。当你意识到自己在抱怨的时候,停下来,问问自己是要变得快乐还是继续这样抱怨下去。

你准备好过没有抱怨,更加快乐的生活了吗?

❧单词注释❧

complain [kəm'plein] *v.* 抱怨，发牢骚；诉说

effectively [i'fektivli] *adv.* 有效地；生效地

due [dju:] *adj.* 应支付的；欠款的；欠的

conscious ['kɔnʃəs] *adj.* 神志清醒的，有知觉的

❧实用句型 & 词组❧

I have nothing to complain of. （抱怨）

They stuck the notice on the wall. （粘贴；张贴）

Don't take any notice of others' comments. （关注；理会）

❧翻译行不行❧

我们可以积极主动的在我们生活中设定目标，然后向着目标进发。

_____

不仅外部的环境让我们抱怨，我们还不断的抱怨我们自己。

_____

停止抱怨要做的第一步，就是想清楚你在抱怨什么。

_____

我的健康我做主
My health, my way

Golf：There's nothing like it!

"贵族运动" 高尔夫

When most people think of golf, they probably think of Tiger Woods jet-setting to golf courses around the world winning **prestigious** tournaments and making a lot of money. *It seems hard to believe that what is now an international sport and multimillion-dollar industry evolved from origins as humble as hitting a pebble around sand dunes with a stick.*

It is generally agreed that golf was first played in Scotland in the 15th century. Its popularity spread throughout the 16th century, and the first international golf match took place in 1682 between players from England and Scotland. Clubs began forming soon after, and concrete rules of the game were **established**.

The Industrial Revolution brought a period of change for golf. Suddenly, with the mass production of golf clubs and balls, the average person could afford to play. New railway lines made it possible for people to go to the country for the day, and thus play on a different **course** every weekend.

Golf was made an Olympic sport in 1900, by which time there were already more than 1,000 golf courses in the United States. The famous PGA was formed in 1916, and by 1944, the equally famous PGA tour consisted of 22 events and was held throughout the year.

Legendary golfers Jack Nicklaus, Arnold Palmer, and Gary Player **dominated** the game from the 60s'into the 70s', wowing fans by winning almost all of the events they competed in. Nicklaus still holds an unbeaten record of five U.S. PGA championships, six U.S. Masters titles, and four U.S. Opens.

These days, it is up to current stars like Tiger Woods and David Duval to keep **spectators** glued to the TV set. Even if you are not a big fan, why not head off to the driving range and have a go? More than 23 million players exist in the United States alone, *and they are all likely to tell you the same thing about golf: There's nothing like it!*

一提到高尔夫球，大多数人可能就会想到泰格·伍兹乘喷气客机到世界各地的高尔夫球场赢得备受瞩目的锦标赛，并大把大把地赚钱。很难相信如今这个价值高达数百万美元的国际性工业，是从随便拿根棍子，在沙丘上挥打鹅卵石这种不起眼的运动发展起来的。

众所周知，高尔夫起源于 15 世纪的苏格兰，普及于 16 世纪。首场国际高尔夫球赛就是在 1682 年举行的，选手均来自英格兰及苏格兰。不久，高尔夫俱乐部开始成立，同时也制定了具体的比赛规则。

工业革命为高尔夫运动带来了一系列的变革。突然间，随着高尔夫球杆及高尔夫球的大量生产，普通百姓也接触到了这项运动。新建的到郊区的火车线路使人们可以在比赛当天往返，因此每个周末可以在不同的球场打球。

1900 年，高尔夫被正式确定为奥林匹克运动项目，那时美国已有上千个高尔夫球场。著名的职业高尔夫球员联盟于 1916 年成立；到 1944 年，同享盛名的职业高尔夫球员联盟巡回比赛，在 1 年内举行了 22 场比赛。

高尔夫球界的传奇人物——杰克•尼克要劳斯，阿诺德•帕尔默及加里•普莱耶一直称霸于 60 到 70 年代的高尔夫球坛。他们几乎囊括了所有的比赛奖项，使球迷们大为赞叹。尼克劳斯至今仍保持数项无人能破的辉煌记录：5 个美国职业高尔夫锦标赛冠军、6 个美国高尔夫精英赛冠军，及 4 个美国公开赛冠军头衔。

现在，高尔夫则靠当红球星泰格•伍兹和大卫•杜瓦的魅力吸引球迷通过电视观看比赛。即使你不是头号球迷，也可以去高尔夫球场挥一挥杆，尝试一下。仅在美国就有 23，000，000 人从事高尔夫运动。关于高尔夫，他们会异口同声地说，"没有比它更好的运动了！"

❧单词注释❧

prestigious [ˌpresˈtiːdʒəs] *adj.* 有名望的，有威信的

established [isˈtæbliʃt] *adj.* 已建立的；已确立的；

course [kɔːs] *n.* 路线；方向

dominate [ˈdɔmineit] *v.* 支配，统治，控制

spectator [spekˈteitə] *n.* 旁观者；目击者

❧实用句型 & 词组❧

George is hard to get along with. （困难的）

The National Day was celebrated throughout the country. （遍及）

What are you up to? （忙于）

❧翻译行不行❧

很难相信如今这个价值高达数百万美元的国际性工业，是从随便拿根棍子，在沙丘上挥打鹅卵石这种不起眼的运动发展起来的。

_____

工业革命为高尔夫运动带来了一系列的变革。

_____

关于高尔夫，他们可能会异口同声地说，"没有比它更好的运动了！"

_____

The True Cigar

恋上哈瓦那雪茄

Even before you come to grips with the cigar itself, there are small pleasures to be enjoyed, starting with the box—an ornately decorated yet **functional** relic from the days before the invention of plastic. A true cigar box is made from cedarwood, which allows the tobacco to breathe and to continue maturing. It is sealed with what looks like a high-denomination bank note (the export warranty of the respective government), and it is often covered with the kind of baroque graphic art that conjures up thoughts of brandy and boudoirs: curlicues, gold embossing, vignettes of white-bosomed ladies and bewhiskered gentlemen, florid typography—everything, in fact, that nineteenth-century pop artists could lay their hands on.

When you open the box, your nose is treated to a classic aroma, a bouquet that deserves a few quiet moments of appreciation before you proceed any further. It is a particularly masculine scent, and men have been known to line their clothes closets with the thin leaves of cedarwood that separate the fat rows of cigars. (The thought of walking around smelling like a human corona may not appeal to all of us, but there are, God knows, worse things to smell of, as anyone who has been ambushed and sprayed on his way through the **cosmetics** department at Bloomingdale's will confirm.)

Now we come to the cigars, looking as **prosperous** and well filled as a group of investment bankers after a killing. This is the beginning of what should be at least forty-five minutes of unhurried enjoyment. Cigars should never be rushed, or puffed absentmindedly while you're doing deals on the phone. The more attention you give them, the more pleasure they will give you, so if you don't have a quiet hour or so, save the cigar until later. The leisurely ceremonial of preparing and smoking one of nature's minor triumphs is worth the investment in time.

A knowledgeable smoker will always inspect his cigar before committing himself. This is not an affectation ; good cigars are made by human hands, which are fallible, and are sometimes stored in unsuitable conditions, which can be fatal. A cigar in its prime will feel firm as you roll it between thumb and index finger, and slightly elastic as you squeeze it. Brittle cigars will not taste good, and should be put aside for less discriminating smokers, such as politicians.

If the cigar pleases your eye, your nose, and your fingers, the next step is to make an incision in the wrapper at the head so that the smoke can be drawn through. Surgical techniques vary from smoker to smoker. Rambo, should he ever do anything as un-American as smoke a Cuban cigar, would probably bite off the end. More delicate souls will use a cigar cutter or even a sharp fingernail to make a small opening. The cut should be clean, and not too deep ; if you stab a cigar in the head with a penknife or a toothpick, you will create a funnel, which results in a hot, bitter smoke.

The last stage before lighting up is optional. Should you remove the band—that miniature work of art just below the head—or should you leave it on? When it was first invented (credit is often given to Gustave Bock, a Dutchman), the band had a **practical** purpose, which was to prevent the outer wrapper from coming adrift as the cigar heated up. Nowadays, with more reliable gumming methods, the risk of losing the wrapper is very slight, so it comes down to a question of aesthetics. Do you prefer your cigars to be decorated or totally nude? Either is fine, and only pedants make a fuss about it.

So you've rolled and you've squeezed and you've sniffed and you've cut, and now you are ready to light up. Once again, a certain finesse is required, and certain laws of nature should be observed. The most important rule is never to use a gas lighter unless you like the taste of gas fumes. Similarly, don't be tempted to lean across the dinner table and gaze into the d é colletage of your beloved as you light up from a candle. Wax and tobacco don't mix. Use a match. When you have the cigar in your mouth, bring the flame close to the end (about one third of an inch away) and rotate it so that you make an even burn that starts at the **rim** and spreads to the center.

You can now settle back and take the first luxurious puff. There is a richness of texture to cigar smoke that makes inhaling quite unnecessary: it is enough just to hold the smoke in the mouth for a few seconds before blowing it gently toward the heavens. And as you watch it hanging in the air, thick and blue gray and aromatic, you can easily imagine that what you are smoking was hand-rolled on a Cuban maiden's long brown thigh. (I doubt that this delightful practice still exists in the cigar factories, but a man can dream.)

"The cigar smoker," wrote Marc Alyn, "is a calm man, slow and sure of his wind." You will never see an experienced cigar man taking quick, agitated puffs. He is concentrating—albeit in a relaxed and sometimes even trancelike fashion—on the pleasure of the moment. This mood of leisurely well-being that is induced by a good cigar is perhaps its greatest attraction. It even has social benefits, because this mild euphoria makes heated argument almost impossible. Nobody but a clod would waste a $45 Havana by waggling it around for emphasis or stubbing it out in anger.

Despite a good cigar's tranquilizing effect, it doesn't kill conversation. *Quite the contrary*, *since it encourages contented and appreciative listeners.* (Why do you think cigars are handed out at the end of formal dinners? Obviously, to render the audience benign, no matter how long and terrible the speeches are.) Stories told over a cigar are funnier, observations are more profound, pauses are comfortable, the cognac is smoother, and life is generally rosier. An hour with a good cigar and a couple of friends is a vacation from life's nonsense.

　　即使你还没把雪茄抓在手里，仍然有一些小小的乐趣可先供自己享受一下。就从雪茄盒开始吧——这是个装饰华丽但不失功能性的盒子，算是塑料发明前的遗迹。真正的雪茄盒子是用杉木做的，可以让烟草透气，继续闷熟。封条看起来像是高面值的银行票据（这是各国政府核发的输出许可证），上面通常还布满了印刷精美的巴洛克风格的图画，叫人想起白兰地酒和美人的香闺：涡卷曲的花纹，镶金的浮雕，柔光照片里露出雪白胸脯的淑女和一脸络腮胡须的绅士。其实，这都是 19 世纪通俗画家笔下的东西，一应俱全。

　　等你打开雪茄盒，一阵隽永的芳香便会扑鼻而来。这份浓郁值得你为之流连片刻，静静体味一番，然后再进行下一步。雪茄香味有一股特别的阳刚气。男人们通常把雪茄储藏在衣橱里，再放一些杉木针叶，把一排排胖嘟嘟的雪茄和衣服隔开，以免串味。(谁都不想自己的古巴雪茄闻起来活像根科罗娜雪茄。其实和变了味的雪茄比起来，这不算什么，比这更糟的是曼哈顿的布鲁明黛尔百货公司的化妆品柜台的香水埋伏，所有经历过的男士都可以出来作证。)

　　接下来，该说说雪茄了。一根根雪茄就像成功的投资银行家在获得暴利之后，大腹便便的样子。这只是刚刚开了个头，紧随其后的，还有至少 45 分钟不慌不忙的享受呢。抽雪茄绝对不能急，也不能一边吞云吐雾，一边分心于手中的电话，与人谈着生意。你越是专心于享用雪茄,雪茄带给你的快乐也就越多。所以，假如你抽不出一小时左右的空闲，让你安安静静地抽上一枝雪茄，那就留待以后再说吧！为了造物主这一小小的杰作投入些时间，从容准备、尽情享用这全套仪式，还是值得的。

内行的烟鬼在吸烟前，一定要检查一下他的雪茄。这可不是装模作样。好的雪茄都是手工制成的，难免会出些差错。有些雪茄也可能贮存的环境不对，那可是致命伤。上等的雪茄夹在食指和拇指间捻动，会觉得十分结实，捏一捏也觉得它略带些微的弹性。松松脆脆的雪茄味道并不好，应该留给分辨能力较差的人，比如政客之流享用。

这雪茄你若是看着养眼，闻着满意，摸起来也舒服，那下一步便是在雪茄头部的外包烟叶上开个切口，好让烟气穿透。动这种外科手术的技巧，因吸烟者不同而相异。像电影《第一滴血》中的兰博这号人，假使他也做出抽古巴雪茄这等最不美国的行为，那他可能就是一口咬掉雪茄的屁股。比较优雅的人则会用雪茄刀，或者尖尖的指甲，划开一个小切口。切口一定要整齐，也不可太深。如果你用刀片或牙签戳雪茄的头，就要小心别弄出个大洞来。那样的话，吸出来的烟会又烫又苦。

点烟之前的最后一步其实是可有可无的。你是要撕掉那一圈带子呢——就是烟头下面的那一圈微型画，还是留着不动？它刚被发明出来的时候可是有实用功效的。这份殊荣归之于一位荷兰人，古斯塔夫博克，雪茄品牌标签的引入者，也是率先涉足古巴雪茄的欧洲人之一，就是要防止雪茄点燃之后，外层卷雪茄的烟叶散落开来。如今，上胶的方法已经比较可靠了，这一层外卷烟叶散掉的风险也就很小了。所以，是否撕掉那一圈带子，不过是美观与否的问题。你是喜欢你的雪茄附着一些装饰物呢，还是想让它一丝不挂？其实两种做法都可行，只有喜欢卖弄的人才会对此小题大做。

好啦，你捻也捻过了，捏也捏过了，闻也闻过了，切也切过了，现在就等着点烟了。还是一样，需要用点技巧，还得遵守一些大自然的规律。而最重要的一条规则就是绝对不要用打火机，除非你喜欢汽油味。同样地，你不可动辄弯腰趴到餐桌上，一边就着蜡烛点烟，一边死死盯着露肩低胸的美人儿。石蜡和烟草是水火不容的，请用火柴。雪茄叼在嘴里之后，将火苗移到雪茄的尾端（保持约 1/3 英寸的距离），环绕一周，让雪茄均匀地从边缘点燃，再燃烧至中央。

现在你可以往后一靠，好好喷出第一口氤氲的烟雾了。雪茄的烟气有醇厚浓郁的质感，所以，没必要吸进去，只消将烟含在嘴里几秒钟，再仰头朝天徐徐吐出即可。当你看着空中灰蓝色的烟雾，浓厚又芬芳，你十有八九会幻想，你正在抽的这根雪茄是由一位古巴少女在她修长的褐色大腿上婆娑卷成的。（我不太确定，这种撩人的做法是不是还流传于现在的雪茄工厂里。但是，男人们做做梦也无妨嘛！）

马可·埃林写道："抽雪茄的人是一个冷静的人，从容不迫、目标明确。"你绝对看不到一个老资格的烟民会焦躁不安、狂吐烟圈的。他一定是专心沉浸在那一刻的喜悦之中。这份专注是轻松的，甚至像是处于一种眩晕的状态。好雪茄带来的这种悠闲、安逸的心情，或许正是它最大的魅力所在。雪茄甚至还有其社交上的好处，因为在这种略微飘飘欲仙的氛围里，几乎不太可能出现激烈的争论。除了笨蛋，有谁还会捏着 45 美元一根的哈瓦那雪茄四处招摇，却只是为了发表一下自己对某一问题的看法呢，又有谁会在一怒之下就将一根点燃的哈瓦那雪茄掐灭了呢？

虽然一枝上等雪茄具有镇静的效用，但还不至于扼杀聊天的雅兴。恰恰相反，正是因为雪茄，造就出了一批批心甘情愿且心悦诚服的听众。（要不然的话，在晚宴结束时，你干吗要发雪茄给大家呢？很清楚啊，就是想要听众慈悲为怀而不管那演讲有多臭、多长。）抽雪茄的时候，听到的故事比平常更好笑，观察比平常更深刻，一时的静默也很舒服，干邑白兰地喝起来更濡滑，生活变得更美好。花一个小时，抽一根好雪茄，还有一两位好友做伴，可以暂且摆脱生活中无谓的纷扰。

雪茄怎么抽

　　众所周知，抽香烟是将烟雾吸入肺部，然后吐出，而抽雪茄与抽香烟截然不同。正确的抽食方法是抽雪茄的同时口含雪茄烟雾，在充分享受雪茄特有的醇香后轻轻吐出烟雾。需注意的是，雪茄的烟灰有助于冷却雪茄，因而，不要轻易弹掉烟灰。最后，当你品尝完一支醇香的雪茄后，不要像熄灭香烟那样将之掐灭，你只需将雪茄放在烟灰缸边，数秒后，它就会自动熄灭。

单词注释

ornately [ɔː'neitli] *adv.* 装饰过分地

cosmetics [kɔz'metiks] *n.* 化妆品，美容品

prosperous ['prɔspərəs] *adj.* 兴旺的，繁荣的

wrapper ['ræpə] *n.* 包裹布；包装纸

nude [njuːd] *adj.* 裸的；与生俱有的

luxurious [lʌg'zjuəriəs] *adj.* 奢侈的；骄奢淫逸的

实用句型 & 词组

He smoked at least half a packet of cigarettes a day. (至少)

He put aside his work to spend more time with his son. (把……放在一边)

They walked a couple of miles. (几个，三两个)

翻译行不行

即使你还没把雪茄抓在手里，仍然有一些小小的乐趣可先供自己享受一下。

当你打开雪茄盒，一阵隽永的芳香便会扑鼻而来。这份浓郁值得你为之流连片刻，静静体味一番，然后再进行下一步。

恰恰相反，正是因为雪茄，造就出了一批批心甘情愿且心悦诚服的听众。

健身误区，——数来

*Physical fitness is today's hot **topic**.* And everywhere you turn your hear something new. But is it all true?

The more you sweat, the more fat you burn

This myth has encouraged people to work out in extreme heat or wear layers of clothes or rubber or plastic weight-loss suits in the hope of sweating fat off. Unfortunately, it's water they're losing, not fat.

Fat burns when it is used as a fuel source for exercise, which doesn't happen initially. When you first begin to exercise, you burn carbohydrates or **sugars**. It takes about 20 minutes of easy to moderate aerobic activity before the transition from burning sugars to fat begins. (Aerobic exercise is any rhythmic and continuous activity that uses oxygen and large muscle masses of the body, such as the arms and legs. Examples are bicycle riding, jumping rope, walking, jogging, aerobic dance, and swimming.) So, to burn the flab, plan on working out at least 40 minutes.

If you stop working out, your muscles will turn to fat

If you decrease your activity and continue to eat the same or more, you may **gain** back that spare tire that you worked so hard to lose. It's not, however, because your muscles turned to fat. Muscles may atrophy or lose their tone, but they won't turn to fat. Muscle is muscle and fat is fat.

Exercise increases appetite

This is true for hard or intense exercise that lasts for 60 minutes or longer. Moderate exercise that is less than 60 minutes, however, will probably **reduce** your appetite for one to two hours.

Exercise always lowers blood sugar

Generally, *exercise will lower blood sugar and it's best to prepare for exercise by eating before you start out.* If your blood-sugar level is above 250 mg/dl, however, exercise could make it rise even higher.

You can get fit in 10 minutes a week

This and similar claims are common, but untrue. There are no shortcuts to getting fit. Becoming fit takes work and the general rule is 20 minutes of **aerobic** activity three times a week. Consistency is the key. If you miss a day or two, don't try to compensate by doing double duty—you open yourself up to injury.

No pain, no gain

Many people tend to overdo their exercise programs looking for quick results. Doing so, however, may prove to be your downfall by resulting in injury or **sore** muscles.

Your best bet is to start any exercise program slowly and gradually increase the workout.

We start people out with 15 minutes of stretching, 30 to 40 minutes of walking or walking/jogging, and end with 10 more minutes of stretching. *This gives people a good beginning without the pain or injury.*

Electric stimulation

Electric stimulation may help make a muscle contract and tone it **slightly,** but this technique can't take the place of exercise, and it certainly won't help you lose weight.

健身是当今的热门话题。无论你走到哪里，都能听到许多新奇的事情。但是，那些都是正确的吗？

流汗越多，消耗的脂肪越多

这个错误的观点鼓励人们在极热的环境下运动，或者穿好几层衣服或者穿橡胶或塑料减肥服，希望通过流汗将脂肪排出。然而，他们排出去的是水而非脂肪。

作为一种燃料能源，脂肪只有运动才能消耗。但在刚开始运动时是不能奏效的。当你开始运动时，你消耗的是碳水化合物，或是糖分。平缓进行有氧运动大约 20 分钟后，才会使你由消耗糖分向消耗脂肪过度。(有氧运动就是有节奏的、持续的活动。它需要耗氧并且锻炼像手臂和腿部的大块肌肉。例如骑自行车、跳绳、步行、慢跑、跳舞和游泳)。所以说，要消耗脂肪，至少要运动 40 分钟。

停止运动，肌肉变脂肪

如果你的运动量减少，但食物的摄入量不变或有所增加，那过去努力锻炼减去的脂肪很可能会卷土重来。然而，这并不是因为你的肌肉变成了脂肪。肌肉可能萎缩或失去弹性，但是它们是不会变成脂肪的。肌肉是肌肉，脂肪是脂肪。

锻炼增加食欲

对于持续进行了 1 个小时或更长时间剧烈运动的人来说确实如此。然而，不到 1 个小时的平缓运动很可能在 1 ～ 2 个小时内降低你的食欲。

锻炼可以降低血糖

在通常情况下，锻炼能降低血糖，在开始锻炼前你最好先吃点东西。然而，如果你的血糖量高于 250 毫克 / 分升，锻炼会使你的血糖量升得更高。

每周 10 分钟，还你健康

这种说法和类似的观点很普遍，但不正确。健康之路无捷径。

要想变得健康就必须锻炼。一般是每周进行 3 次，每次 20 分钟的有氧运动。关键是要坚持。如果你中间耽误了一两天，不要通过加倍的运动来弥补——这样做你会受到伤害的。

不劳则无获

有些人倾向于过度锻炼以期快速见效，然而，这样做可能会造成伤害或引起肌肉疼痛。

最好的方式就是缓慢地开始锻炼，然后逐渐增加运动量

我们让人们开始锻炼时，先用一刻钟的时间进行伸展运动，然后进行 30 ～ 40 分钟的步行或步行加慢跑，最后以 10 分钟的伸展运动结束。以这样的方式开始运动就会有个良好的开端，不会感到疼痛，也不会受到伤害。

用电疗代替锻炼

电疗能帮助肌肉变得结实些，但是这种疗法代替不了锻炼，也减不了肥。

❧单词注释❧

topic ['tɔpik] *n.* 题目；话题；论题

sugar ['ʃugə] *n.* 糖

gain [gein] *v.* 得到；获得，赢得

reduce [ri'djuːs] *v.* 减少；缩小；降低

aerobic [ˌeiə'rəubik] *adj.* 需氧的；有氧的

sore [sɔ] *adj.* 痛的，疼痛发炎的

slightly ['slaitli] *adv.* 轻微地；稍微地；微小地

❧实用句型 & 词组❧

Can you work out on the map where we are now?（确定）

He started out to write a novel.（着手进行）

We'll try to improve our teaching methods.（努力）

❧翻译行不行❧

健身是当今的热门话题。

在通常情况下，锻炼能降低血糖，在开始锻炼前你最好先吃点东西。

以这样的方式开始运动就会有个良好的开端，不会感到疼痛，也不会受到伤害。

Watch Out for the Hot Tea

烫茶，小心！

*The British Medical Journal study found that drinking steaming hot tea has been linked with an **increased** risk of oesophageal cancer.*

Experts said the finding could explain the increased oesophageal cancer risk in some non-Western **populations**.

Adding milk, as most tea drinkers in Western countries do, cools the drink enough to **eliminate** the risk.

Tobacco and alcohol are the main factors linked to the development of oesophageal cancers in Europe and America.

Golestan Province in northern Iran has one of the highest rates of OSCC in the world, but rates of smoking and alcohol consumption are low and women are as likely to have a diagnosis as men. Tea drinking, however, is widespread.

The University of Tehran researchers studied tea drinking **habits** among 300 people diagnosed with OSCC and compared them with a group of 570 people from the same area.

Nearly all participants drank black tea regularly, on average drinking over a litre a day.

Compared with drinking warm or lukewarm tea (65℃ or less), drinking hot tea (65-69℃) was associated with twice the risk of oesophageal cancer, and drinking very hot tea (70℃ or more) was associated with an eight-fold increased risk.

The speed with which people drank their tea was also important. There was no association between the amount of tea **consumed** and risk of cancer.

Drinking a cup of tea in under two minutes straight after it was poured was associated with a five-fold higher risk of cancer compared with drinking tea four or more minutes after being poured.

A large proportion of Golestan inhabitants drink hot tea, so this habit may account for a substantial **proportion** of the cases of oesophageal cancer in this population.

Previous studies from the UK have reported people prefer their tea to be about 56-60℃—cool enough not to be risky.

Oliver Childs, a spokesman for Cancer Research UK, said, "Tea drinking is part of many cultures, and these results certainly don't point to tea itself being the problem. But they do provide more evidence that a regular habit of eating and drinking very hot foods and drinks could increase your risk of developing cancer of the oesophagus." *He advised tea-drinkers to* **simply** *wait a few minutes for their brew to cool from* "scalding" *to* "tolerable" .

《英国医学期刊》发表的研究表明，喝滚烫的茶水会增加患食道癌的风险。

专家表示，这一发现解释了非西方国家的人们患食道癌的人数有所增加这个现象。

西方国家的人喝茶时习惯加牛奶，这样可以降低茶水的温度，从而降低患癌的风险。

在欧美国家，抽烟和喝酒是导致食道癌的主要原因。

伊朗北部的格列斯坦省是世界上食道癌发病率最高的地区之一。虽然当地居民抽烟喝酒的比例都不高，但是无论男女，发病率都很高。因为，当地的居民都有饮茶的习惯。

德黑兰大学的专家们研究对比了 300 名食道癌患者与 570 名来自相同地域的普通人的饮茶习惯。

几乎所有的参与者都有喝红茶的习惯，并且平均每人每天至少饮用一公升。

与饮用较热茶或温茶（65 度或以下）的人相比，引用热茶（65–69 度）的人患食道癌的危险性要高出两倍。一旦水温超过 70 度，患病的风险将增加 8 倍。

而饮茶的速度也至关重要。而喝多少茶则与患癌无关。

在茶沏开两分钟之内就开始饮用的人，比等茶沏开后四分钟或更久才喝的人患食道癌的危险要高出 5 倍。

由于格列斯坦省的居民有饮热茶的习惯，所以当地人患食道癌的比例一直都很高。

先前英国人的一项调查显示，他们更喜欢饮用温度在 56 度至 60 度之间的茶水，这样明显降低了患食道癌的危险。

英国癌症研究所的发言人奥利弗·查尔德表示，饮茶已经成为许多国家文化的一个组成部分。很明显，喝茶本身并没有错。但是越来越多的证据表明，食烫物和喝热饮的饮食习惯的确会增加患食道癌的风险。他建议人们在沏茶后等上几分钟，待滚烫的茶水降到适宜的温度后再喝。

健康饮茶小贴士

忌空腹饮茶，茶入肺腑会冷脾胃；忌饮烫茶，最好是 56℃ 以下；忌饮冷茶，冷茶寒滞、聚痰；忌冲泡过久，防止氧化、受细菌污染；忌冲泡次数多，茶中有害微量元素会在最后泡出；忌饭前饮茶，茶水会冲淡胃酸。

单词注释

increase [in'kriːs] *v.* 增大；增加；增强

population [ˌpɔpjuˈleiʃən] *n.* 人口

eliminate [i'limineit] *v.* 排除，消除

habit ['hæbit] *n.* 习惯

consume [kənˈsjuːm] *v.* 消耗，花费；耗尽

proportion [prəˈpɔːʃən] *n.* 比例；比率

simply ['simpli] *adv.* 简单地，简易地；简明地

实用句型 & 词组

Computers are now in widespread use.（广泛的）

I didn't want to be associated with it at all.（使有联系）

The law provides that these ancient buildings must be preserved.（规定）

翻译行不行

《英国医学期刊》发表的研究表明，喝滚烫的茶会增加患食道癌的风险。

_____

而饮茶的速度也至关重要。而喝多少茶则与患癌无关。

_____

他建议人们在沏茶后等上几分钟，待滚烫的茶水降到适宜的温度后再喝。

_____

The Relations Between PH and Body Weight
如何做个碱性人

The risk

No doubt you've heard of the increasingly popular "raw food" and "whole food" diets. Why are people so interested in eating raw food or whole food? One reason is that eating these types of food reduces the risk of **acid** accumulation in your body.

Raw and whole foods are usually digested more efficiently than cooked and refined foods. When we cook foods, we destroy the natural enzymes that are part of the food in its raw form. These enzymes were intended by nature to help us digest the food. When we consume food without these natural enzymes, our bodies either digest the food improperly or allow an excessive amount of nutrients to be absorbed into the bloodstream.

In both instances, the result is obesity. When too many nutrients are absorbed at once, the body converts the excess glucose into fat. Improperly digested food moves slowly through the digestive tract, where it becomes increasingly acidic. To protect its vital organs from this acidic waste, the body converts the acid into fat and stores it safely away from the organs.

Chemical additives in processed foods make the situation worse. These chemicals confuse the appetite mechanism that tells us when we've had enough to eat. *Processed foods also upset the digestive cycle.* The body will either identify these foods as allergens and then store them safely away from the organs as fat, or the **remnants** of undigested food will become acidic and enter the bloodstream as acid waste.

The damage

Acid waste that is not converted into fat remains in the bloodstream, where it sticks to the blood vessel walls and blocks the passage of vital oxygen and nutrients headed for the body's cells. The body's metabolism becomes sluggish, and the result is weight gain and obesity.

If the metabolism continues to grow sluggish, all of the body's organs are potentially affected. Degenerative disease sets in. Cells die, acid continues to accumulate, and the cycle repeats on a more damaging scale.

The accumulation of acid in the digestive **tract** makes digestion increasingly inefficient. When that happens, even healthy foods can become acidic and the food allergies will become more prevalent. Undigested food allergens will continue to be deposited in fat cells, leading to greater obesity. Because acidity disrupts the body's chemistry, the hormones needed to convert fat into fuel also fail to function properly, so the obesity persists no matter how healthy your diet becomes.

The benefits of a balanced pH

To stop this vicious circle in its tracks, you need to consume food and supplements that will neutralize the acid already accumulated in your body. You also need nutrients that will help restore your body's hormonal balance. Eating the right types of raw and whole foods in the right sequence can help.

It's also important to restore your enzyme balance so that your digestive system will work properly again. Proper digestion means that you will crave less food, accumulate less acid waste, convert less of your food intake into fat cells, and create additional digestive enzymes.

To set this positive spiral in motion, you need to identify and eliminate the foods that cause acid elevation and consume the foods that increase enzyme production. This will help restore the pH balance in your digestive system and will make a significant contribution to your overall health.

If you truly want to change and help your body heal itself you need to take a **proactive** approach. Don't expect to feed your body processed foods, not exercise, then pop a pill and be all better? it just doesn't work that way. If you want to bring your body into pH balance then you need a complete approach.

风险性

你一定听说过，现在"生鲜食物"和"天然食物"的饮食方式已经越来越流行了。为什么现在的人们会对生鲜食物和天然食物如此感兴趣呢？这其中的一个原因是：吃这些食物可以减少人体内酸性物质的积累。

生鲜和天然的食物通常比烹饪过的、精制的食物更容易被人体吸收。在烹饪过程中，食物中酶的原本结构就被破坏了。而这些酶是帮助我们消化食物的。当我们吃了没有那些天然酶的食物时，我们的身体要么是无法正确地消化食物，要么会让过量的营养物质进入到血液中。

这两种情况导致的结果都是肥胖。当一次性吸收过多的营养的时候，身体就会把多余的葡萄糖转化为脂肪。没有被正确消化的食物在消化道中缓慢移动，然后酸性变得越来越强。为了防止重要的器官被这些酸性垃圾腐蚀，我们的身体就把这些酸转化成脂肪储存起来，达到与重要的器官隔离的目的。

加工食物使用的化学添加剂会使这种情况更加糟糕。这些化学物质会影响我们的食欲——它告诉我们什么时候才算吃饱了。加工过的食物也会影响我们的消化循环。我们的身体同样会认为这些食物是过敏原，并把它们以脂肪的形式储存起来，以免损害重要的器官，否则这些残余的未消化的食物会变成酸性物质进入血液。

危害性

未转化成脂肪的酸性垃圾会留在血液当中，粘附在血管壁上，阻塞氧气及营养物质到达细胞的通道。于是身体的新陈代谢减慢，导致体重增加和肥胖。

如果新陈代谢持续减慢，那么我们身体的所有器官都会受到潜在的危害。病变开始发生。细胞死亡，酸继续积累，并在这样的循环中增加损伤的规模。

酸的积累使消化道的消化功能下降。到这个时候，甚至健康的食物都会被转化成酸性物质，食物过敏会越来越严重。食物过敏会继续增加脂肪的储存，并导致更严重的肥胖。由于酸会破坏人体所需的化学反应，激素转化脂肪成为能量的反应就无法正常进行，这时无论多么健康的饮食都无法阻止你继续肥胖了。

合理 pH 值的好处

要阻止这种恶性循环，你需要吃一些食物和补品来中和体内积累的酸。你同样需要一些营养物来恢复激素的平衡。适当吃一些生鲜和天然的食物会帮助你恢复健康。

恢复酶的功能也同样重要，这样你的消化系统才能再次正常的运行。正常的消化意味着渴望更少的食物，积累更少的酸，转化更少的食物为脂肪，生成更多的消化酶。

要让这个积极的状况运转，你需要识别和除去那些能够增加酸的食物，吸收能增加酶的食物。这能够帮助你维持消化系统 pH 值的平衡，并为你的健康做出贡献。

如果你真的需要改变或帮助你身体的自我治疗，最好要提前预防。经常吃加工过的食物，不锻炼身体，不要以为吃一些药片就能够万事大吉。这是没有用的。如果你想维持身体 pH 值的平衡，一个完整的方案是非常有必要的。

身体"酸化"其实挺难

　　在正常的生理状态下，人体酸碱失衡并不容易发生。一旦人体的 pH 值低于 7.35，就属于酸中毒了。酸中毒早期常表现为食欲不振、恶心、呕吐、腹痛等症状，进一步发展可表现为嗜睡、烦躁不安、精神不振，以致昏迷死亡。如果你真的属于所谓的"酸性体质"，那赶紧上医院，找大夫进行专业治疗吧。

❧单词注释❧

acid ['æsid] *adj.* 酸的，有酸味的

remnant ['remnənt] *n.* 残余，剩余；遗迹

cell [sel] *n.* 细胞

enzyme ['enzaim] *n.* 酶

proactive [ˌprəu'æktiv] *adj.* 积极主动；提前行动

❧实用句型 & 词组❧

She's potentially our best player, but she needs to practice much harder. （潜在地；可能地）

That is not, properly speaking, a dictionary, but a grammar. （严格地）

Our goal is to eliminate poverty. （排除，消除）

❧翻译行不行❧

生鲜和天然的食物通常比烹饪过的、精制的食物更容易被人体吸收。

_____

加工过的食物也会影响我们的消化循环。

_____

恢复酶的功能也同样重要，这样你的消化系统才能再次正常的运行。

_____

Tree Pose

Stretches hips, inner thighs ;strengthens legs, spine, core

1. *Stand with your legs and feet together*, *hands on hips.* **Transfer** weight to your left foot as you bend the right knee and place the sole of the right foot on the inside of your left leg (beginners start at the ankle ;more advanced yogis, raise the right foot to the inside of the left thigh). Gently press the right foot against the left leg.

2. Bring the palms of your hands together in front of the heart in prayer pose. Hold for 1 minute on each side. More advanced yogis: Raise your arms straight directly overhead, palms facing in.

Boat Pose

Strengthens core, psoas, quadriceps

1. Sit with knees bent, feet flat on the floor. **Lean** back slightly so you're balancing on your sit bones. *Raise your legs so shins*

are parallel to the floor, knees bent.

2. Extend arms forward, parallel with the floor, palms facing each other. Keeping your chest high and your core engaged, begin to **straighten** your legs. *Hold for 5 to 10 breaths. Repeat 5 times.*

Garland Pose

Stretches low back, groin, hips, ankles

1. Stand with feet slightly wider that hip–width. Bring the palms of your hands together in front of your heart in prayer pose. Turn toes out slightly.

2. Deeply bend the knees, squatting down between your legs. Keeping palms together, gently press your elbows to the insides of your knees, opening up the hips. Keep the spine long, chest open. Feel tension in the lower back begin to melt away. Hold for at least 1 minute.

Half Lord of the Fishes

Stretches hips, shoulders, back, neck ;strengthens spine

1. Sit on the floor with legs outstretched in front of you. Bring the sole of the right foot on the floor outside of the left hip (right knee points to the ceiling).

2. Bend the left knee and bring the left foot to the outside of the right hip. Place right hand on the floor just behind your right hip. Lift your left arm to the **ceiling**. As you exhale, bend the left arm and place the left elbow to the outside of your right knee.

3. Lengthen your spine with each inhale and twist deeper with each exhale. Press the left elbow into your right leg to help revolve the **upper** body more and more. Look to the wall behind you. Hold for 5 to 10 deep breaths. Repeat on the opposite side.

Bridge Pose

Stretches front of body ;strengthens hamstrings, gluteus

1. Lying on your back, bend your knees and place the soles of your feet flat on the floor about hip—width apart. Toes point straight to the wall in front of you. Place arms straight along your sides, palms down.

2. Gently press into your feet as you raise hips to the sky. Allow the front of your body to slowly expand with each breath. Hold for 5 to 10 breaths. Repeat 3 times.

树式

拉伸臀部、大腿内侧，强健腿部、脊椎和核心肌群

1. 双腿和双脚并拢站立，双手放在臀部。将身体重心转移到左脚，右膝弯曲，将右脚脚掌放在左腿内侧（初学者开始时可以先放在脚踝处，层次高的瑜伽练习者可以将右脚放在左边大腿的内侧）。慢慢将右脚向左腿压。

2. 手掌合十放在胸前，成祈祷状。保持这个姿势一分钟。层次高的瑜伽练习者：双臂伸直并举过头顶，手心相对。

船式

强健核心肌群、腰肌和四头肌

1. 屈膝坐，双脚平放在地面上。身体微微向后仰，以坐骨来保持平衡。双腿抬起，使小腿和地面平行，双膝弯曲。

2. 双臂向前伸直，与地面平行，掌心相对。挺胸，使核心肌群也得到锻炼，然后伸直双腿。保持这个姿势呼吸五到十次，重复这个动作五次。

花环式

拉伸下背部、腹股沟、臀部和踝关节

1. 双脚分开站立，比臀部略宽。手掌合十放在胸前，成祈祷姿势。脚趾微向外撇。

2. 双膝弯曲，蹲在双腿间。手掌合十，慢慢地将手肘紧贴双膝内侧，臀部张开。脊椎挺直，胸部打开。感到下背部的张力开始消失，保持这个姿势至少一分钟。

半鱼王式

拉伸臀部、肩部、背部、颈部，强健脊椎

1. 双腿向前伸直坐在地上，将右脚脚掌放在左臀部的外侧（右膝指向天花板）。

2. 左膝弯曲，左脚放在右边臀部的外侧。将右手放在右边臀部后面的地上，抬起左臂。呼气时弯曲左臂，将左肘放在右膝的外侧。

3. 吸气时脊椎挺直，呼气时让脊椎加剧扭曲。左肘向右腿方向顶，帮助上半身加大扭转幅度。向你身后的墙的方向看。保持这个姿势深呼吸五到十次。换另一侧重复这个动作。

桥式

伸展上半身，强健腿筋和臂肌

1. 仰卧，屈膝，脚掌平放在地面上，大致与臀部同宽。脚趾正对着你前方的墙。双臂伸直放在身体两侧，掌心向下。

2. 臀部向空中抬起，同时双脚轻轻地发力。每次呼吸时上半身慢慢伸展。保持这个姿势五到十次，并重复三次。

瑜伽与一般运动的不同

瑜伽：必须集中意识，在一定时间内保持某种姿势，从而达到身心的统一。瑜伽有平衡内分泌，使身体四肢均衡发展的功效。且能保持全身舒畅，心灵平静，内在充满能量；恢复体力，不需要太长的时间。

一般运动：使身体机械式的不停地运动，无需用意识。能使肌肉发达，但不均衡。体力易消耗，肌肉易疲劳，需要长时间睡眠以恢复体力。

❧单词注释❧

transfer [træns'fə:] *v.* 搬；转换；调动

lean [li:n] *v.* 倾身，屈身

straighten ['streitn] *v.* 把……弄直；使挺直

ceiling ['si:liŋ] *n.* 天花板；顶篷

upper ['ʌpə] *adj.* 较高的；上面的；上首的

opposite ['ɔpəzit] *adj.* 相反的，对立的

❧实用句型 & 词组❧

The fight against inflation has been going on for almost two years. （违反）

He is engaged in his business. （从事）

He is suffering from nervous tension. （紧张）

❧翻译行不行❧

双腿和双脚并拢站立，双手放在臀部。

_____

双腿抬起，使小腿和地面平行，双膝弯曲。

_____

保持这个姿势五到十次，并重复三次。

_____

Arthritis All–clear for High Heels

高跟鞋，我为你平反

Fears that wearing high–heeled shoes could lead to knee arthritis are unfounded, say researchers.

But being overweight, smoking, and having a **previous** knee injury does increase the risk, the team from Oxford Brookes University found.

They looked at more than 100 women aged between 50 and 70 waiting for knee surgery, and found that choice of shoes was not a factor.

The study was published in the *Journal of Epidemiology and Public Health.*

More than 2% of the population aged over 55 suffers extreme pain as a result of osteoarthritis of the knee.

The condition is twice as **common** in 65–year–old women as it is in men the same age.

Women's and men's knees are not biologically different, so the researchers wanted to find out why twice as many women as men develop osteoarthritis in the joint.

*Some researchers have **speculated** that high-heeled shoes may be to blame.*

The women in the study were quizzed on details of their height and weight when they left school, between 36 and 40 and between 51 and 55.

They were asked about **injuries**, their jobs, smoking and use of contraceptive hormones.

However, while many of these factors were linked to an increased risk over the years, tottering around in high heels for years was not.

研究人员称，人们害怕穿高跟鞋会导致膝盖关节炎是没有根据的。

牛津布鲁克斯大学研究小组发现，肥胖、吸烟或者以前膝盖受过伤会增加得关节炎的危险。

他们对年龄在 50 ～ 70 岁之间的 100 名将要做关节手术的妇女进行了调查，发现鞋子并不是导致关节炎的原因。

该研究发表在《流行病学与公共卫生》杂志上。

55 岁以上的人群中有超过 2% 的人忍受着膝盖关节炎带来的极度痛苦。

这种情况在 65 岁的妇女中发生的几率是同龄男性的两倍。

女性和男性的膝盖在生理上并没有什么不同，所以研究者们想知道为什么患关节炎的女性人数是男性的两倍。

有研究者推测高跟鞋可能是罪魁祸首。

参加该项研究的妇女们被详细询问了她们在毕业时、36 到 40 岁之间，51 到 55 岁之间的身高和体重。

研究人员还询问了她们的受伤、工作、吸烟和使用避孕激素的情况。

然而，多年来，许多因素都增加了患关节炎的危险，但是常年穿着高跟鞋走路并不是原因之一。

选择高跟鞋之必读攻略

俗话说，鞋穿在脚上，舒不舒服只有自己知道，对于高跟鞋而言，更是如此，要兼顾美观及舒适，并非想像中那么简单。

A. 入门级：5~7 厘米。对女性来说，5~7 厘米是最受欢迎、最安全的美丽高度，特别是 5.5 厘米的鞋跟，性感、易行走。

B. 进阶级：10 厘米。10 厘米的高跟鞋很具诱惑性，尤其是细跟晚装鞋，大多都是这个高度。

C. 专业级：14 厘米。近年来坡跟鞋的大热，令高跟鞋屡创新高，14 厘米超高跟鞋是 Chanel 设计师 Karl Largerfeld 认为最适合与超迷你裙搭配的款式，能够令全身线条更加修长，让女人产生超性感的魅力。

单词注释

previous ['priːvjəs] *adj.* 先的，前的，以前的

common ['kɔmən] *adj.* 普通的；常见的

speculate [ə'spekjuˌleit] *v.* 思索；沉思；推测

injury ['indʒəri] *n.* 伤害；损害

regular ['regjulə] *adj.* 规则的，有规律的；固定的；正常的

实用句型 & 词组

Smoking can lead to lung cancer. （导致）

The publishing house has published five dictionaries. （发行）

The man detailed to us all the wonders he had seen in his travels.（详细说明）

翻译行不行

研究者称，人们害怕穿高跟鞋会导致膝盖关节炎是没有根据的。

_____

有研究者推测高跟鞋可能是罪魁祸首。

_____

然而，多年来，许多因素都增加了患关节炎的危险，但是常年穿着高跟鞋走路并不是原因之一。

_____

Sitting Around Is Bad For Your Heart

动一动，心脏更健康

A new study from the Journal of Medicine and Science in Sport and Exercise says if your bottom spends too much time parked in a chair, your heart pays a **heavy** price. *It finds the more hours of what's called "sitting time" over the course of your day, the more time for **blockages** to clog up your arteries.* Let's take a typical eight-hour shift. let's say you're sitting less than two hours, or a quarter of your day. Well in that case, you're probably OK. But when half of your day is spent taking a load off your risk of heart **disease** goes up about twelve percent. Spend six hours of that frozen in a chair, and the risk zooms up by more than a third. *And if your eight hours is **basically** eight hours of desk work. It Jumps more than fifty percent higher*. So how can you st and up and fight the war against "sitting time". Well, number one, take the stairs, not the elevator. *Take walking breaks, not coffee breaks.* let your legs do the walking. Don't e-mail, go speak to a co-worker in person. And if you need to use the restroom, choose the one that's farthest away. And finally, take a walk rather than eating **lunch** at your desk.

《体育科学与运动医学杂志》发表的一项新研究称，如果你的屁股在椅子上坐太长时间，你的心脏会为此付出沉重代价。这项研究发现，一天之内所谓的"坐立时间"越长，动脉阻塞的时间就越长。以普遍的 8 小时工作制来说，如果说你坐的时间少于两小时，或者说少于一天的四分之一，如果是这样的话，你的健康是没有什么问题的。但当你有半天的时间都是坐着时，那么你患上心脏病的风险大概会增加 12%。如果你有 6 个小时动也不动地坐在椅子上，那么你患心脏病的风险会增加三分之一以上。如果你的 8 小时基本上都是坐在办公桌前工作，那么你患心脏病的风险会跃升到 50% 以上。那么你怎样行动起来与"坐立时间"相抗争呢？首先，爬楼梯而不是坐电梯。休息时间散散步而不是喝咖啡。让你的双腿走走路。不要发邮件，亲自走到同事跟前交谈。如果你要去洗手间，选择最远的那个。最后，走路去吃午餐而不是坐在办公桌前吃午餐。

单词注释

heavy ['hiːvi] *adj.* 重的，沉的

blockage ['blɔkidʒ] *n.* 封锁；妨碍

disease [di'ziːz] *n.* 病，疾病

basically ['beisikəli] *adv.* 在根本上

lunch [lʌntʃ] *n.* 午餐

实用句型 & 词组

He traveled in all quarters of the earth when he was young. （地方，地域）

We haven't much time, please speak to the subject. （提及）

You have finished, haven't you? In that case, you may have a rest. （既然那样）

翻译行不行

这项研究发现，一天之内所谓的"坐立时间"越长，动脉阻塞的时间就越长。

_____

如果你的 8 小时基本上都是坐在办公桌前工作，那么你患心脏病的风险会跃升到 50%以上。

_____

休息时间散散步而不是喝咖啡。

_____

时尚达人
Look to those fashion icons

The First Lady—Michelle Obama

美国第一夫人米歇尔·奥巴马的华丽转型

*Elegant, passionate, a strong career woman and a **devoted** mom, Michelle Obama has already become a role model with an army of fans as she prepares to become the nation's first lady.*

Three days after celebrating her 45th birthday, she will take her place by her husband's side on Jan 20 as Barack Obama is sworn in as the nation's first African-American president.

Obama will be one of the nation's youngest first ladies after the graceful Jackie Kennedy, who was just 31 when John F. Kennedy took office.

And while she has insisted that her main job will be "mom-in-chief" to her two daughters, Malia, 10 and Sasha, 7, her role may well **evolve** in the months ahead as the first family settles into the White House.

*Officially Michelle Obama has said she has no **political** ambitions of her own*, and resigned from her job as vice-president at the University of Chicago medical center, where she worked for 7 years.

"Even as first lady, my number one job would still be mom," she told reporters just before the Nov 4 elections. "My first priority will always be to ensure that our daughters stay grounded and healthy, with normal childhoods—including homework, dance and soccer."

*"One of the great **challenges** for Michelle Obama is she is going to have to juggle many balls, wear many hats,"* historian Robert Watson said.

"She's going to have to be a wife, a mother, but also the first lady. And this is a woman who is used to having a very successful, high-powered career and it's an **enormous** challenge."

He added, "My sense is that Michelle Obama probably comes better prepared to handle these challenges than any first lady in history. The reason is that she has sort of been super woman."

"First lady" is an unofficial title bestowed on the **hostess** of the White House. Helped by a staff of around 100, she has many largely ceremonial duties and accompanies the president to state functions and on trips.

她优雅大方、充满热情，她是成功的职业女性，是位称职的母亲，在即将成为美国第一夫人时，米歇尔·奥巴马已经拥有了一大批"粉丝"。

在过完 45 岁生日后的第 3 天，米歇尔将于 1 月 20 日正式成为美国第一夫人，这一天她的丈夫巴拉克·奥巴马将就任，成为美国首位非裔总统。

米歇尔将成为继端庄优雅的前第一夫人杰奎琳·肯尼迪之后美国历史上最年轻的第一夫人，肯尼迪就任美国总统时，杰奎琳年仅 31 岁。

尽管米歇尔一直表示她将做个"全职妈妈"，照顾好两个女儿——10 岁的玛利亚和 7 岁的萨沙，但当这个第一家庭入主白宫后，她的角色在今后的几个月将不可避免地发生变化。

米歇尔曾公开表示自己没有什么政治抱负。她已辞去芝加哥大学医学中心副主任一职，她在那里工作已有 7 年之久。

米歇尔在去年 11 月 4 日大选前夕接受记者访问时说："即使成为第一夫人，我的首要任务仍将是做个称职的妈妈，让我们的女儿健康快乐地成长，过一个正常的童年——让她们（和其他孩子一样）每天做家庭作业，去跳舞，踢足球。"

历史学家罗伯特·沃特森说："米歇尔面临的最大挑战之一就是如何处理好各种角色。"

"她既是妻子、母亲，又是第一夫人。她曾是一位成功的职业女性，'第一夫人'对于她来说是个不小的挑战。"

他说："与历届第一夫人相比，我感觉米歇尔可能会是面对这些挑战时准备最充分的一位。因为她有点女强人的感觉。"

"第一夫人"是对白宫女主人的一个非官方的称呼。在约 100 名员工的协助下，第一夫人要处理很多仪式性的事务，还要陪同总统出席各种国事活动和访问各国。

❧单词注释❧

devoted [di'vəutid] *adj.* 献身的；虔诚的；专心致志的

evolve [i'vɔlv] *v.* 使逐步形成；发展，展开

political [pə'litikəl] *adj.* 政治的；政治上的

challenge ['tʃælindʒ] *n.* 挑战；邀请比赛

enormous [i'nɔ:məs] *adj.* 巨大的，庞大的

hostess ['həustis] *n.* 女主人

❧实用句型 & 词组❧

She is a graceful dancer. （典雅的）

Two people were ahead of us, and travelling fast. （领先，占先）

He will probably refuse the offer. （很可能）

❧翻译行不行❧

她优雅大方、充满热情，她是成功的职业女性，是位称职的母亲，在即将成为美国第一夫人时，米歇尔·奥巴马已经拥有了一大批"粉丝"。

_____

米歇尔曾公开表示自己没有什么政治抱负。

_____

米歇尔面临的最大挑战之一就是如何处理好各种角色。

_____

Oprah Named Entertainment's Most Powerful Woman

"脱口秀女王" 奥普拉

The Hollywood Reporter on Friday named Oprah Winfrey the most powerful woman in entertainment on its annual "Power 100 List."

Winfrey, whose "Oprah" talk show began in national **syndication** *22 years ago, played a role in the victory of President-elect Barack Obama by endorsing him early in his run and by supporting him throughout the campaign.*

Elizabeth Guider, editor of *The Hollywood Reporter*, remarked on Winfrey's "immense cultural influence" and said she could be "the most influential woman in America."

Winfrey, 54, jumped from the No. 6 spot on the entertainment trade paper's 2007 list to No. 1 this year. The Hollywood Reporter noted that a study by University of Maryland economists found Winfrey's support for Obama won him more than 1 million votes **nationwide**.

Winfrey's production company, Harpo Inc., made $345

million last year. She oversees an empire that includes her TV show, a magazine and an online store.

Anne Sweeney, president of Disney–ABC Television Group, was given the No. 2 spot on the list after coming in top a year ago. *Sweeney oversees her company's news, entertainment and daytime divisions, along with its cable and publishing* **branches**.

Amy Pascal, chairman of Sony Pictures Entertainment Motion Picture Group, won the No. 3 spot on the list.

Other women listed included actress Angelina Jolie, at No. 24, who has bolstered her public image with philanthropic endeavors ;*comedian Tina Fey, No. 51 in part for playing Sarah Palin, the 2008 Republican vice presidential nominee, in wildly popular TV impersonations during the election* **campaign** ;and 16-year-old pop star Miley Cyrus, who has a Disney franchise built around her and rounded out the list at No. 100.

The Top 10 in the Women in Entertainment Power 100 list are ;

1. Oprah Winfrey, chairman of Harpo Inc.

2. Anne Sweeney, president of Disney–ABC Television Group and co-chairman of Disney Media Networks.

3. Amy Pascal, chairman of Sony Pictures Entertainment Motion Picture Group and co-chairman of Sony Pictures Entertainment.

4. Nancy Tellem, president of CBS Paramount Network Television Entertainment Group.

5. Stacey Snider, co-chairman and CEO of DreamWorks.

6. Bonnie Hammer, president of NBC Universal Cable Entertainment and Universal Cable Productions.

7. Judy McGrath, chairman and CEO of MTV Networks.

8. Mary Parent, chairman of MGM Worldwide Motion Picture

Group.

9. Dana Walden, chairman of 20th Century Fox Television.

10. Nina Tassler, president of CBS Entertainment.

《好莱坞记者报》于上周五公布了本年度娱乐界"百位最具影响力女性"排行榜，奥普拉·温弗瑞荣登榜首。

奥普拉在 22 年前开始主持面向全国播出的"奥普拉脱口秀"节目，在今年的总统大选中，她为奥巴马获胜助了一臂之力，这位名嘴在竞选之初就公开表示支持奥巴马，并在整个竞选活动中一直支持他。

《好莱坞记者报》编辑伊丽莎白·盖德称奥普拉具有"巨大的文化影响力"，并说她会成为"全美国最具影响力的女性"。

54 岁的奥普拉从 2007 年该娱乐榜的第 6 位跃至今年的首位。该报称，马里兰州立大学的经济学家开展的一项研究表明，奥普拉的支持为奥巴马在美国赢得了 100 多万张选票。

去年，奥普拉成立的制作公司"哈泼集团"赢利 3.45 亿美元，她的这个"传媒帝国"不仅制作她的脱口秀节目，还经营杂志和网上商店等业务。

去年的排行榜冠军、迪斯尼 –ABC 电视集团总裁安妮·斯威妮今年屈居第二。她掌管着公司的新闻、娱乐、日间节目、有线服务和出版等业务。

索尼影视娱乐集团董事长艾米·帕斯卡尔位列第三。

其他上榜的女性还包括：安吉丽娜·朱莉（第 24 位），她的乐善好施使其公众形象大幅提升；喜剧演员蒂娜·菲（第51位），她因总统大选期间在一档收视率很高的模仿秀节目中模仿副总统候选人莎拉·佩林而人气飙升；流行小天后米莉·赛洛斯（第100位），这位年仅16岁的小天后因出演迪斯尼热门剧一炮走红。

今年娱乐界十大最具影响力女性如下：

1. 奥普拉·温弗瑞，哈泼集团董事长。

2. 安妮·斯威妮，迪斯尼-ABC电视集团总裁，迪斯尼传媒电视网副董事长。

3. 艾米·帕斯卡尔，索尼影视娱乐电影集团董事长，兼索尼影视娱乐有限公司副董事长。

4. 南希·特勒姆，CBS派拉蒙电视娱乐集团总裁。

5. 斯塔西·斯奈德，梦工场副总裁兼首席执行官。

6. 邦妮·哈默，NBC环球有线娱乐制作集团总裁。

7. 朱迪·麦格拉思，MTV电视网董事长兼首席执行官。

8. 玛丽·帕伦特，MGM全球电影集团董事长。

9. 达那·沃尔登，20世纪福克斯集团董事长。

10. 妮娜·塔斯尔，哥伦比亚广播公司娱乐部总裁。

❧单词注释❧

syndication [ˌsindi'keiʃ ən] *n.* 企业联合组织化
nationwide ['neiʃ ənwaid] *adj.* 全国范围的；全国性的
branch [brɑ:ntʃ] *n.* 树枝；支流
campaign [kæm'pein] *n.* 战役；运动，活动

❧实用句型 & 词组❧

Many senators endorsed the new bill. （认可）
His endeavors to get the bill passed failed. （尽力）
Last week，the price of food jumped. （猛增）

❧翻译行不行❧

奥普拉在 22 年前开始主持面向全国播出的"奥普拉脱口秀"节目，在今年的总统大选中，她为奥巴马获胜助了一臂之力，这位名嘴在竞选之初就公开表示支持奥巴马，并在整个竞选活动中一直支持他。

_____

她掌管着公司的新闻、娱乐、日间节目、有线服务和出版等业务。

_____

她因总统大选期间在一档收视率很高的模仿秀节目中模仿副总统候选人莎拉·佩林而人气飙升。

_____

The Most Popular Model Laetitia Casta
最受欢迎的模特：拉蒂夏·卡斯特

Laetitia Maria Laure Casta was born on May 11, 1978 in Port-Audemer in Normandy, France. Her childhood was spent in Normandy's countryside—playing in the rivers and the woods with her older brother. *Back then, she was such a* **tomboy** *that she was often mistaken for a little boy.*

When she was fifteen, Laetitia was discovered while vacationing with her family on a beach in Corsica. She was making sand **castles** with her little sister when a photographer for Madison Models approached her. He handed her father a business card and an invitation to bring his daughter to Paris for some test shots. *Suspicious at first, her parents* **eventually** *caved to Laetitia's pleas.*

Within weeks of her first shoot,she was walking the runway for Jean Paul Gaultier. Having never worn make-up, she screamed when she caught her reflection in the mirror. But anyway, by the time she was sixteen, she had landed three magazine covers.

Until she turned 21, Laetitia lived at home with her parents. Now she shares an apartment in London with her older brother, Jean-Baptistie. Her favorite activities include painting, writing, going to the cinema, go-carting with her brother and dancing to disco music. *Proving not to be just a **pretty** face, Laetitia holds a brown belt in Judo.*

拉蒂夏·卡斯特于 1978 年 5 月 11 日生于法国诺曼底的 PortAudemer。她的童年生活是在诺曼底的乡下度过的——跟她哥哥在河流、森林中嬉戏。那时候她顽皮得不像个女孩子，所以经常有人将她误认成男孩。

拉蒂夏是在 15 岁那年被星探发现的，当时她和家人在科西嘉的海滩度假。她和妹妹正在堆沙子城堡的时候，一个为麦迪森模特公司工作的摄影师走近了她。他将名片递给拉蒂夏的父亲，并邀请他带拉蒂夏去巴黎试镜。尽管开始拉蒂夏的父母有些半信半疑，但是后来还是架不住拉蒂夏的苦苦哀求，接受了摄影师的邀请。

在她初次露面的前几周里，她在 T 型台上为 Jean paul Gaultier 这个牌子展示服装。因为她以前从来没有化过妆，所以当她看到镜子里的自己时，忍不住尖叫了起来。但不管怎么说，到了 16 岁的时候，拉蒂夏已经成了三份时装杂志的封面女郎。

拉蒂夏 21 岁之前都和父母一起生活。现在她和哥哥 Jean-Baptiste 一起住在伦敦的一家公寓里。她最喜欢的活动包括画画、写作、看电影、和哥哥玩微型赛车以及跟着迪斯科音乐跳舞。为了证明自己不仅只有张漂亮脸蛋，拉蒂夏还是个配有褐带的三段柔道手。

"模特"一词的来源

英文为"Model"，模特在体型、相貌、气质、文化基础、职业感觉、展示能力等方面都具备一定条件，并对服装设计、制作与面料、配件以及音乐、舞台灯光等具有良好的领悟能力。

模特，英文 Model，被解释为"模型"、"模式"、"模特儿"。如果一个人具有了某种商业使用目的，他/她就成为了 Model。

❀单词注释❀

tomboy ['tɔmbɔi] *n.* 男孩似的顽皮姑娘

castle ['kɑ:sl] *n.* 城堡

eventually [i'ventjuəli] *adv.* 最后，终于

pretty ['priti] *adj.* 漂亮的；秀丽的；可爱的

❀实用句型 & 词组❀

The lost bike was discovered at the bus stop. （找到）

He cautiously approached the house. （靠近）

The gang was screaming for the immediate release of their leader.
（强烈要求）

❀翻译行不行❀

那时候她顽皮得不像个女孩子，所以经常有人将她误认成男孩。

_____

尽管开始拉蒂夏的父母有些半信半疑，但是后来还是架不住拉蒂夏的苦
苦哀求，接受了摄影师的邀请。

_____

为了证明自己不仅只有张漂亮脸蛋，拉蒂夏还是个配有褐带的三级柔
道手。

_____

As a boy growing up in Shenyang, China, I practiced the piano six hours a day. I Loved the instrument. At first I played on clunky Chinese keyboards — cheap, but the best we could afford. Later my parents bought me a Swedish piano, but I broke half the **strings** on it playing Tchaikovsky. That's when my parents and my teacher decided I was too much for such an instrument — and for our hometown. *To be a serious musician, I would have to move to Beijing, our cultural capital.* I was just eight years old.

My father, who played the erhu, a two-stringed **instrument**, made a great sacrifice. To relocate to Beijing with me, he quit his concertmaster's job, which he loved, and my mother stayed behind in Shenyang to keep working at her job at the science institute to support us.

Suddenly my father and I were newcomers — outsiders. To the others around us, we spoke with funny northern accents. The only apartment we could find for the money we had was in an unheated building, with five families sharing one bathroom. My father cooked, cleaned and looked after me. He became a housewife, **basically**.

We lived far from my school, and since the bus was too expensive, my father would "drive" me on his bicycle every day. It was an hour-and-a-half trip each way, and I was a heavy boy, much heavier than I am as an adult. He did this in winter too. Imagine! During the coldest nights, while I practiced piano, my father lay in my bed so it would be warm when I was tired.

I was miserable, but not from the **poverty** or pressure. My new teacher in Beijing didn't like me. "You have no talent," she often told me, "You will never be a pianist." And one day, she "fired" me.

I was just nine years old. I was devastated. I didn't want to be a pianist anymore, I decided. I wanted to go home to my mother. For the next two weeks I didn't touch the piano. *Wisely, my father didn't push. He just waited.*

Sure enough, the day came at school when my teacher asked me to play some holiday songs. I didn't want to, but as I placed my fingers on the piano's keys, I realized I could show other people that I had **talent** after all.

That day I told my father what he'd been waiting to hear — that I wanted to study with a new teacher. From that point on, everything turned around.

I started winning competitions. It was soon clear I couldn't stay in China forever. *To become a world-class musician, I had to play on the world's big stages.* So in 1997, my father and I moved again, this time to Philadelphia, so I could attend The Curtis Institute of Music. Finally our money worries were easing.

The school paid for an apartment and even lent me a Steinway. At night, I would sneak into the living room just to **touch** the keys.

Now that I was in America, I wanted to become famous, but my new teachers reminded me that I had a lot to learn. I spent two years practicing, and by 1999 I had worked hard enough for fortune to take over. The Chicago Symphony Orchestra heard me play and liked me, but orchestra **schedules** were set far in advance. I thought I might join them in a few years.

The next morning, I got a call. The great pianist Andre Watts, who was to play the "Gala Benefit Evening" at Chicago's Ravinia Festival, had become ill. I was asked to substitute. That performance was, for me, the moment. After violinist Isaac Stern introduced me, I played Tchaikovsky's Piano Concerto No. 1. My father's mouth hung open throughout the **entire** song.

Afterward, people celebrated — maybe they were a bit drunk — and asked me to play Bach's Goldberg Variations. So I played until 3:30 a.m. I felt something happening. Sure enough, gigs started pouring in. Lincoln Center, Carnegie Hall. Still, my father kept telling me, "You'd better practice!"

我小时候在中国的沈阳市生活,每天都花6个小时练习弹钢琴。我喜欢这种乐器。一开始我弹的钢琴是国产的,样子笨重但却便宜,是我们能买得起的最好的钢琴。后来我父母给我买了一架瑞典钢琴,于是我就用这架钢琴练习柴可夫斯基的曲子，可是半数的琴弦都弹断了。这时我父母和老师认为这样的乐器以及我的家乡已经不再适合我了。要成为一名真正的音乐家，我得去我们的文化之都——北京。那年我才8岁。

我的父亲弹奏一种二弦乐器——二胡，他为我做出了巨大的牺牲。为了带我到北京，他辞去了自己热爱的首席乐师的工作，我的母亲则留在沈阳的科研所继续工作以维持我们的生活。

突然间父亲和我成了"新移民"——外地人。对周围的人来说，我们说话带着滑稽的北方口音。我们的钱不多，只能租得起没有供暖的居民楼，与5家共用一个卫生间。我父亲做饭、打扫卫生还照顾我。他基本上成了一个"家庭主妇"。

我们的住处离学校很远，乘公交车太贵，父亲就每天"驾驶"自行车送我去学琴，单程就需要一个半小时，我当时还很胖，体重比我现在还重。一年四季，天天如此，真不敢想象啊！当我在数九寒天的夜里练琴时，父亲就躺在我的床上，这样等我累了就可以睡在暖和的被窝里了。

我那时的心情很糟糕，并不是因为贫困或压力，是因为我在北京的新老师不喜欢我。"你没有天赋，"她经常对我说，"你永远成不了钢琴家。"一天，她把我"开除"了。

我当时才9岁，这对我的打击太大了。我决心不要当什么钢琴家了。我想回家，我想妈妈。接下来的两个礼拜我都没有碰钢琴。我父亲很明智，并没有强迫我，只是在等我回心转意。

果不其然，一天上学，老师叫我演奏一些节日的曲子。我本来不想弹，但当手指一碰到琴键时，我就意识到我能向别人展示自己，我是有天赋的。

那天我告诉父亲他一直在等待的那句话——我想跟一个新老师学琴。从那一刻起，一切都有了转机。

我开始在多项比赛上获奖。我很快就清晰地意识到：我不能永远呆在中国。要想成为世界级音乐家，就必须在世界的大舞台上演奏。所以，在1997年，父亲和我又一次搬迁，这次搬到了费城，我在那里的柯蒂斯音乐学院求学。我们终于不用再为钱伤神了。学院出钱为我租了公寓，甚至借给我一架施坦威钢琴。在夜里我会悄悄溜进起居室，只为摸摸琴键。

既然来到美国，我就想成名，但是我的新老师们提醒我还有很多东西要学。我练了两年的琴，到1999年我已苦练到时来运转的程度。芝加哥交响乐团听了我的演奏，很欣赏我，但是乐团的表演日程是提前安排好的。我认为得过几年才能加入这个乐团。

第二天早上我接到了一个电话。著名钢琴演奏家安德烈·沃茨身体不适，他本来要在芝加哥拉维尼亚音乐节演奏"节日义演之夜"。乐团叫我去顶替他。那场演出铸就了我的辉煌。小提琴演奏家艾萨克·斯特恩把我介绍给了听众，我演奏了柴可夫斯基的《第一钢琴协奏曲》。从开始演奏到曲终，我父亲一直乐得嘴都合不拢。

之后人们就开始庆祝——可能他们有点醉了——还让我演奏巴赫的《哥德堡变奏曲》。于是我弹到了凌晨3点半。我感到有了某种突破。果然，演奏的工作机会不断涌来，林肯中心、卡内基音乐厅。可是我父亲仍然告诫我："你要多练！"

❧单词注释❧

string [striŋ] *n.* 线；细绳；带子

instrument ['instrumənt] *n.* 仪器；器具，器械

basically ['beisikəli] *adv.* 在根本上

poverty ['pɔvəti] *n.* 贫穷，贫困

talent ['tælənt] *n.* 天才，天资

touch [tʌtʃ] *v.* 接触，碰到

schedule ['ʃedjuːl] *n.* 表；清单；目录

entire [in'taiə] *adj.* 全部的，整个的

❧实用句型 & 词组❧

I have to go right now. (必须，不得不)

Dodge is waiting to have a word with you. (等待)

She took me wrong. (领会)

❧翻译行不行❧

要成为一名真正的音乐家，我就得去我们的文化之都——北京。

_____

我父亲很明智，并没有强迫我，只是在等我回心转意。

_____

要想成为世界级音乐家，就必须在世界的大舞台上演奏。

_____

How to Become a Remarkable Speaker

跟奥巴马学演讲

You might say that one reason Barack Obama is president of the US is because he knows how to give a good speech. In 2004, a little-known senator from Zllinois gave the keynote speech at the Democratil National Convention. That senator was Obama .It was a **remarkable** speech—poetic, and inspiring. The people who heard it would remember it for a long time.

Since 2004, Obama has written and delivered thousands of speeches. these are usually praised for two reasons: he treats the audiences like intelligent adults, and he is able to express complicated ideas in a **straightforward**, natural way.

Before becoming president, Obama was a lawyer, a college professor, and a successful writer—his two memoirs have become best-sellers. The skills he needed to succeed in his previous jobs have also contributed to his success as a speechmaker.

As a lawyer, Obama learned how to make strong, convincing

arguments. As a professor, he learned how to explain complex subjects in ways that helped students understand without boring them. As a writer, he learned how to use language to have a powerful impact on his audience. Star musician will. i. am. even turned one of Obama's early speeches into a song during the election campaign.

Obama delivers speeches to audiences large and small. He can make his audiences laugh or cry. His speeches are always thoughtful, well written, and just right for each **occasion**.

Secret weapon

Teleprompter: Obama doesn's go anywhere without his Teleprompter, The textbook-sized panes of glass holding the president's prepared remarks follow him wherever he goes to speak.

Writing team: Obama has a team of people who write his speeches. The writers chat with Obama for hours about what he wants to say. They listen to recordings of past presidential addresses and seek advice from advisers. Obama usually edits and rewrites the **drafts** several times.

Obama's tricks for a lighthearted speech that stays on message:

Make fun of the guests: Obama starts his speech by gently teasing his guests. His opening lines grab the audience's attention while giving them an opportunity to relax and laugh at themselves and each other.

Make fun of yourself: A good rule for speechmakers: If you're going to make a joke about someone else, be sure to make one about yourself, too. Obama mocks his own poor choices for filling the position of Commerce Secretary, saying, "No

President in history has ever named three Commerce Secretaries this quickly." In fact, his first two nominees for the position withdrew their names for different reasons. In a process that had otherwise gone **smoothly**, the Obama Administration was tripped up by the problem of filling the Commerce seat.

你也许会认为，奥巴马之所以能当选美国总统，要归功于他杰出的演讲才能。在 2004 年的一次民主党全国代表大会上，一位名不见经传的伊利诺伊州参议员发表了主题演讲。那个参议员便是奥巴马。那是一场十分精彩的演讲——诗一般的语言充满了振奋人心的力量，令人过耳难忘。

从 2004 年至今，奥巴马已创作发表了数千场演说。这些演讲屡获赞扬的原因大致可归结为两点：一、他将观众视为有智慧的成年人来对待；二、以直率自然的方式来表达复杂难懂的理念。

在当选总统前，奥巴马曾做过律师、大学教授。他还是一位成功的作家，他的两本回忆录都非常畅销。正是这些早年在工作中锻炼出来的技能，使他成为一名成功的演说家。

身为律师，奥巴马懂得如何在辩论中给出令人信服的有力论据。而身为教授，他明白如何将复杂的事物以清晰易懂的方式向学生解释清楚。同时身为作家，他更精通如何用语言打动观众。著名流行乐团黑眼豆豆的灵魂人物 will.i.am，甚至将奥巴马早期竞选的一篇演讲改编成了一首歌。

奥巴马在各种的场合都发表过演说。他既能使人捧腹大笑，也能催人泪下。无论在什么场合，他的演讲总是那么得体，思想与文笔交相辉映。

奥巴马的秘密武器

提词器：无论去哪里，奥巴马都随身携带提词器。每次外出演讲，他都会带着这个笔记本大小的方形玻璃装置，里面有备好的演讲摘要。

写作团队：该团队专门负责为奥巴马撰写演讲稿。演讲前，他们会和奥巴马座谈数小时，充分了解他想要 表达的内容。之后，他们还要听过去的总统演讲录音，并向顾问寻求建议。奥巴马通常会对草稿 进行数次编辑改写。

如何在轻松愉快的演讲中传达你的信息？奥巴马自有妙招：

打趣来宾：奥巴马经常在演讲一开始打趣来宾。这样一来，他的开场白不仅能成功吸引听众的注意力，还可以让他们放松下来，彼此会心一笑。

拿别人开涮的同时，也别忘了自嘲：对一个演讲者而言，如果你想要拿其他人打趣，那么一定别忘了也要自嘲一下。奥巴马曾嘲笑自己在商务部长提名上没有太多选择，他说："在这么短的时间内任命 3 位商务部长，恐怕我是头一个了。"实情是，前两位被提名者都由于种种原因而推掉了。结果任命商务部长这么一件本应很顺畅的事，却成了奥巴马政府的老大难。

🍂单词注释🍂

remarkable [ri'mɑ:kəbl] *adj.* 值得注意的；非凡的；卓越的

straightforward [streit'fɔ:wəd] *adj.* 一直向前的；径直的

occasion [ə'keiʒən] *n.* 场合，时刻；重大活动

smoothly ['smu:ðli] *adv.* 平滑地；流畅地

🍂实用句型 & 词组🍂

Education delivered him from ignorance. （解脱；释放）

He didn't contribute one idea to the document. （贡献，提供）

Children should listen to their parents. (听从，听信)

🍂翻译行不行🍂

你也许会认为，奥巴马之所以能当选美国总统，要归功于他杰出的演讲才能。

_____

身为律师，奥巴马懂得如何在辩论中给出令人信服的有力论据。

_____

拿别人开涮的同时，也别忘了自嘲：对一个演讲者而言，如果你想要拿其他人打趣，那么一定别忘了也要自嘲一下。

_____

Jackson Dies, But The Beat Goes on

杰克逊——是非一生，余响永存

While his elaborate, stop-on-a-dime dance moves and sensual soprano may have influenced generations of musicians, Michael Jackson stood for much more than pop greatness—or tabloid weirdness.

He influenced artists ranging from Justin Timberlake to Madonna, from rock to pop to R&B even to rap, across genres and groups that no other artist was able to unite.

Jackson entered the public consciousness as an **impossibly** cute, preteen wonder in 1969, an unbelievably precocious singer in his family band, The Jackson 5. Even then, his dance moves, borrowed from the likes of James Brown and Jackie Wilson, were exquisite, *and his onstage presence outshone seasoned **veterans***.

The spotlight began to dim when he entered his late teens. However, when he met producer Quincy Jones, the musical landscape changed.

The album Thriller, produced by Jones, became his greatest success and his career-defining achievement. Selling more than 50 million copies, the album was the globe's best-selling disc. The impact was **measured** much more than in stats.

Jackson broke MTV's color barrier. He became the first black artist to be prominently featured on that young, rock-oriented channel when the success of Billie Jean and Beat It became so overwhelming it could not be ignored. He also established a benchmark for the way videos would be made—with stunning cinematography and precision choreography that recalled great movie musicals.

But as Jackson's fame grew, his eccentricities—from his strange affinity for children and childish things to his, at times, asexual image to his **fascination** with plastic surgery—began to dull the shine of his sparkling image.

If his plastic surgery made him disturbingly unwatchable, soon, allegations of child abuse would make him reviled by many. He was overwhelmed with legal and financial troubles and went into seclusion after the trial for child molestation ended in 2005.

A comeback seemed to be most unlikely. But when he announced he'd be doing a series of comeback concerts at London's famed O2 Arena, not only did the initial dates sell out immediately, the demand was so **insatiable** he was signed on for an unprecedented 50 shows. He was expected to embark on a worldwide tour sometime after the concert series was completed in March.

Of course, there will be no comeback now, no Jackson 5 reunion, no new music to share with millions of fans. But the legacy he leaves behind is so rich, so deep, that no scandal can torpedo it. *The "Thriller" may be gone, but the thrill will always remain.*

　　以他忽动忽静的炫丽舞步和令人颤栗的性感高音，迈克尔·杰克逊影响了一代又一代的音乐人。这个名字所代表的，远不止是流行巨星，或小报怪人。

　　从贾斯汀·汀布莱克到麦当娜，从摇滚到流行再到 R & B 甚至饶舌乐，迈克尔·杰克逊对当代歌手、音乐流派、类型风格的影响可谓无人能及。

　　杰克逊进入公众视线始于 1969 年，当时不满 13 岁的他被视为一个可爱的奇迹，是家庭乐队"杰克逊五兄弟"中天才型的早慧歌手。早在那时，他模仿詹姆斯·布朗和杰基·威尔森等歌手的舞蹈动作就近乎完美。他的舞台表演甚至让许多乐坛老将都相形见绌。

　　然而好景不长，渐渐长大的杰克逊在 20 多岁时一度陷入低潮。直到遇见知名制作人昆西·琼斯，他的音乐之路才开始转变。

　　由琼斯制作的专辑《颤栗》是杰克逊最成功的作品，也是他职业生涯的巅峰。该专辑销量超过 5,000 万，该唱片勇夺全球销量桂冠，但《颤栗》的影响远不止这些。

　　杰克逊还打破了 MTV 的种族隔阂。专辑中歌曲《比莉·简》和《走开！》的大肆走红让以针对年轻人和摇滚乐为主的 MTV 频道无法忽视。因此，杰克逊成为首位登上该频道的黑人歌手。

此外，他还树立了音乐电视的制作基准——要像大型歌舞片一样具备完美的摄影技术和精准的舞蹈编排。

但是，随着杰克逊名气的增长，他的很多怪癖——从对儿童和孩子气事物的迷恋，到他塑造的无性形象再到对频繁的整形手术的狂热，使他闪亮的明星光环黯淡不少。

如果说整形手术让他变得惨不忍睹，那么接踵而来的娈童案则让他成了众矢之的。当时的他完全被法律和财务纠纷击溃了。于是，他在 2005 年娈童案结束后毅然选择了隐居。

几年隐居生活之后，杰克逊似乎不太可能复出乐坛了。然而，当他宣布将在伦敦著名的 O2 体育场举办复出演唱会后，不仅最初几场的门票即刻售空，巨大的需求缺口迫使他又加签了 50 场，演出场数之多，无人能及。在三月份的系列演唱会结束后，他便开始着手世界巡演了。

至此，不会再有他的复出演唱会了，也不会再有"杰克逊五兄弟"的团聚了，更不会有新作品与数百万粉丝一起分享了。但是，他留给我们的回忆既丰富又深刻，任何丑闻都不能将之摧毁。那个唱着《颤栗》的"怪人"杰克逊走了，但他曾带给我们的震撼将永存人心。

🌿单词注释🌿

impossible [im'pɔsəbl] *adj.* 不可能的，办不到的

veteran ['vetərən] *n.* 老兵；老手；富有经验的人

measure ['meʒə] *v.* 测量；计量

fascination [fæsi'neiʃ(ə)n] *n.* 魅力；有魅力的东西

insatiable [in'seiʃəbl] *adj.* 永不满足的；贪得无厌的

🌿实用句型 & 词组🌿

I couldn't sleep for exquisite pain. (尖锐的)

One of the survivors needed plastic surgery. (整形手术)

This move made headlines worldwide last year. (遍及全球的)

🌿翻译行不行🌿

他的舞台表演甚至让许多乐坛老将都相形见绌。

由琼斯制作的专辑《颤栗》是杰克逊最成功的作品，也是他职业生涯的巅峰。

那个唱着《颤栗》的"怪人"杰克逊走了，但他曾带给我们的震撼将永存人心。

Justin Timberlake Named Most Stylish Man in America 型男贾斯汀·汀布莱克

Grammy-winning pop singer Justin Timberlake has topped GQ magazine's list of the "10 most Stylish Men in America," and gives his banker stepfather the **credit** for his dress sense.

The men's magazine praised Timberlake, 28, for his impact on fashion, his willingness to take risks and "knack for targeting trends" including hats, three-piece suits, skinny ties and beards.

The timing of the award is good news for Timberlake. William Rast, the clothing line he and friend Trace Ayala launched in October 2006, is on the runway at this week's New York Fashion show for its second outing.

Timberlake said in the March issue of GQ that he got his **sense** of style from his stepfather, Paul Harless, a banker who laid out his suit for the next morning every night and went to work looking "like Richard Gere in *American Gigolo*."

*As for his signature style of wearing a suit with sneakers, Timberlake said it was more a matter of practicality than **design**.*

"I just put sneakers on because I couldn't dance in the shoes I had. I couldn't leap with just insoles and dress shoes. I would've hurt myself," said Timberlake, who rose to fame as a singer with the boy band 'N Sync and went **solo** in 2002.

Other honorees on the list of "Stylish Men" include music producer Mark Ronson, who took second place, and photographer Alex Lubomirski, who was third.

They were joined by rappers Kanye West and T.I., actor Jason Schwartzman and **hotelier** Andre Balazs.

　　日前，"格莱美奖"得主、流行歌手贾斯汀汀布莱克在《GQ》杂志评选出的"全美十大型男"中拔得头筹，他称自己的衣着品味得益于身为银行家的继父。

　　这本男士杂志大赞 28 岁的贾斯汀对时尚的影响力，他那敢于冒险的精神及其引领流行趋势的能力，如他的帽子、三件套西装、窄版领带及蓄胡须等。

　　对贾斯汀来说，这一殊荣来的正是时候。当时他与好友特雷西·阿亚拉于 2006 年 10 月创办的时装品牌 William Rast 正在纽约时装周上进行第二轮展示。

　　贾斯汀在《GQ》三月号中称，他的时尚品味受到继父保罗哈利斯的影响。身为银行家的保罗·哈利斯每晚都会选好第二天要穿的衣服，然后"穿得像电影《美国舞男》中的理查·基尔一样"去上班。

对于自己西装配运动鞋的标志性风格，贾斯汀称这更多考虑的是实用性而不仅是美观。

贾斯汀说："之所以穿运动鞋，是因为我穿别的鞋没法跳舞。穿着时装鞋再垫上鞋垫我没法跑跳自如，那样会受伤的。"贾斯汀在担任"超级男孩"乐队的主唱时一举成名，并于2002年单飞。

其他上榜的"型男"包括音乐制作人马克•朗森和摄影师亚历克斯•路波米斯基，他们分列排行榜第二和三位。

此外，说唱歌手坎耶•维斯特和克利夫•哈里斯、演员詹森•舒瓦兹曼和酒店业大亨安德鲁•巴拉兹也跻身该榜。

超级男孩子

超级男孩组建于1995年。团体的名称据说是由贾斯汀的母亲取的，她在第一次听到五人的和声演唱后，对于他们的声音是如此"同步"（in sync）印象深刻，因此就取名为"'N Sync"。而团名也被认为是取自五位团员的名字：JustiN、ChriS、JoeY、LansteN和JC。

🌿单词注释🌿

credit ['kredit] *n.* 赊账，赊欠；(经济上的) 信誉

sense [sens] *n.* 感觉；意识；观念

design [di'zain] *v.* 设计；构思：绘制

solo ['səuləu] *n.* 独奏曲；独唱曲；独奏

hotelier [həu'teliə(r)] *n.* 旅馆老板；旅馆经营者

🌿实用句型 & 词组🌿

The book made a great impact on its readers. (作用)

Father and his partner launched into a new business. (积极投入；猛力展开)

The position suits with his abilities. (彼此协调)

🌿翻译行不行🌿

这本男士杂志大赞 28 岁的贾斯汀对时尚的影响力，他那敢于冒险的精神及其引领流行趋势的能力，如他的帽子、三件套西装、窄版领带及蓄胡须等。

_____

对于自己西装配运动鞋的标志性风格，贾斯汀称这更多考虑的是实用性而不仅是美观。

_____

其他上榜的"型男"包括音乐制作人马克·朗森和摄影师亚历克斯·路波米斯基，他们分列排行榜第二和三位。

_____

From Vagrant to Hollywood's Favorite

冉冉升起的广告新星

The newest sensation at the center of Hollywood's fashion scene isn't a famous designer or starlet. It's a 56-year-old homeless man who spends his days dancing on roller skates.

John Wesley Jermyn has been a **fixture** in West Los Angeles for more than 20 years. Nicknamed "The Crazy Robertson" and "The Robertson Dancer," he is a constant presence on a stretch of Robertson Boulevard that has become the city's trendiest shopping corridor and a prime strolling spot for tourists and movie stars. Among locals and online, there's much speculation about Mr. Jermyn's personal history, including one oft-repeated rumor that he's a secretive millionaire.

In a plot twist worthy of Tinseltown, Mr. Jermyn now has a clothing label named after him. Since it was introduced last month, 'The Crazy Robertson' brand of T-shirts and sweatshirts, created by a trio of 23-year-olds, has flown off the shelves at Kitson, a haunt of tabloid stars like Paris Hilton. The clothes feature stylized images of Mr. Jermyn, including one design—available on a $98 hoodie—that has a graphic of him dancing and the phrase 'No Money, No Problems' on the back. At the largest of Kitson's three boutiques on Robertson, shirts bearing Mr. Jermyn's likeness are sold alongside $290 'Victoria Beckham' jeans and $50 baby shoes designed by pop star Gwen Stefani.

The label's owners, who grew up in Beverly Hills, have created a MySpace page for Mr. Jermyn. It doubles as an ad for the clothing brand and their nightclub-promotion venture, which is also named "The Crazy Robertson." The young entrepreneurs spent months trying to forge a relationship with Mr. Jermyn— who now goes by the name John Jermien—before gaining his **approval**. They have consulted him on design decisions and had a photographer shoot him for publicity images.

In May, Mr. Jermyn agreed to a deal that entitles him to 5% of "net profit'from clothing sales, according to a copy of the contract seen by The Wall Street Journal. He signed the contract, without speaking to an attorney or family members. But so far he has refused to accept much cash, preferring to be paid in food, liquor and paper for his art projects, according to Teddy Hirsh, one of the label's founders. "He tries not to involve money in his daily life," says Mr. Hirsh, who says he is Mr. Jermyn's agent and manager for future endeavors.

Mr. Hirsh says Mr. Jermyn has already received several small payments, even though the company hasn't "made much profit" so far. "We haven't collected anything for ourselves," says Mr. Hirsh.

Mr. Jermyn's slide into homelessness is a painful subject for his sister Beverly. And so is the clothing deal. She believes "The Crazy Robertson'founders are exploiting her brother's condition to build their brand. I think these guys saw an opportunity and they took it," she says. "I am not happy with the **arrangement**."

Ms. Jermyn, who lives close to the alley where Mr. Jermyn sleeps, says her brother has a form of schizophrenia. He refuses to take medication, she says, despite suffering from fits of shouting and cursing. In the years since his condition began deteriorating in the late 1970s, "he slipped through my fingers like sand," says Ms. Jermyn, 64, who manages facilities for Oracle Corp.

In the late 1980s she testified in court in a proceeding to force her brother to seek help, but psychological evaluators found him "lucid and gracious," according to Ms. Jermyn. She has made countless attempts to provide him with shelter and therapy, and she still visits him twice a week with food. She also pays for his cellphone and collects his Social Security checks on his behalf.

The repackaging of Mr. Jermyn as a fashion front man comes at a time of increased fascination with homelessness. The producers of "Bumfights" — a collection of videotaped street battles between vagrants — claim to have sold more than 300,000 DVDs since 2002, and a British TV series called "Filthy Rich and Homeless" made headlines this year for its depiction of real-life millionaires posing as London beggars.

Across the U.S., a growing number of homeless people have gained attention through the Internet. More than 17,500 videos on YouTube are tagged with the word "homeless." Leslie Cochran, a street resident in Austin, Texas, who has twice run for mayor, has 10,775 "friends" on his MySpace page. *In Boston, the profile* of Harold Madison Jr. — *a homeless man better known as "Mr. Butch" — rose through online clips and a Web site made in his honor.*

Mr. Jermyn was raised in Hancock Park, a historic L.A. neighborhood that's home to some of the city's wealthiest families. His father managed one of L.A.'s largest Chevrolet dealerships.

A star athlete in high school, Mr. Jermyn was **selected** by the Kansas City Royals in the 1969 Major League Baseball draft. He attended Pepperdine University and played a season for a Los Angeles Dodgers' minor-league team in Bellingham, Wash. (He hit just .205 and made 12 errors in 63 games, according to the Society for American Baseball Research.)

Joel John Roberts, chief executive of People Assisting the Homeless, which provides shelters for L.A.'s street residents, says the branding of Mr. Jermyn is "like designing a line of clothing patterned after Iraqi refugees fleeing the war."

Mr. Hirsh and Vic Ackerman, one of the other founders of the clothing line, are sensitive to Ms. Jermyn's concerns about her brother, but say Mr. Jermyn "specifically asked" them not to contact her about the clothing line or the contract. They view Mr. Jermyn as a "business partner" and say they make sure he's aware of how his image is being used.

"He knows everything that's going on," says Mr. Ackerman, noting that Mr. Jermyn nixed a set of promotional photos because he didn't like his outfit and thought he "looked a little puffy."

In conversation, Mr. Jermyn speaks softly and mixes short, lucid sentences with longer, less coherent remarks. He has been arrested more than a dozen times since 1986 for violations such as trespassing and jaywalking, according to court records. Most of his skating and curb-side dancing now takes place near Robertson Boulevard, but in the past he roamed throughout Beverly Hills and West L.A., often cradling a boombox and shimmying to loud music. "He was always an extraordinary dancer," says Jim Horne, a classmate of Mr. Jermyn's at Los Angeles Baptist High School.

In addition to his sister, Mr. Jermyn speaks regularly with Ginny Berliner, a 64-year-old woman who befriended him when she owned an antique shop on Robertson. Mrs. Berliner, who now lives in Maryland, used to pay for Mr. Jermyn to sleep in a motel and covered his monthly coffee bill at Michel Richard, the well-known patisserie. "He wants notoriety and glory, but he can't accept money," she says.

On a recent afternoon, clad in his trademark black leggings and visor, Mr. Jermyn said he is "a facilitator" for the brand, and hopes it will expand into music or film. He has become a one-man marketing team, **plastering** company stickers and pictures of himself on a wall that faces pedestrians on Robertson.

At Kitson's boutiques and on its Web site, the first shipment of "Crazy Robertson" women's clothes—about 35 items—sold out in three days, and the store immediately ordered about 90 more pieces, according to owner Fraser Ross. Many of the online buyers were not from Los Angeles and presumably not familiar with Mr. Jermyn, he says. The brand may have appeal beyond L.A., says Mr. Ross, because its name includes "Robertson," which like Rodeo Drive is a destination associated with **glamorous** shopping.

Mr. Hirsh says the success at Kitson has already generated

interest from other retailers. He calls Mr. Jermyn "our Michael Jordan" and is looking into a trademark for "the Crazy Robertson" name and logo.

Ms. Jermyn, meanwhile, has different hopes. "I don't want to see my brother get hurt," she says. "They're taking advantage of someone who is very vulnerable and very trusting."

毫无疑问，好莱坞是引领时尚潮流的中心，而眼下，这个时尚中心最吸引人们眼球的并不是某位知名设计师或是崭露头角的新星，而是一位整天穿着溜冰鞋跳舞的 56 岁流浪汉。

他叫约翰•韦斯利•杰梅恩，他在洛杉矶西区已经呆了 20 多年。人们给他起的绰号有"疯狂罗伯逊"、"罗伯逊舞蹈家"，因为他常常在西洛杉矶最新潮的购物区罗伯逊大街一带游荡，而这里也是游客和影视明星最爱光顾的地方。关于杰梅恩的个人背景，当地人和互联网上有不少传闻，其中流传甚广的一个说法是，他虽然外表寒酸，其实身家百万。

杰梅恩为"疯狂罗伯逊"品牌拍摄的宣传照看上去满离奇的。不过，杰梅恩的名字现在跟一个服装品牌密不可分，这个名为"疯狂罗伯逊"的品牌是上个月推出的，产品是 T 恤衫和运动衫，是由三位 23 岁的小伙子创立的。一经问世，该品牌就在 Kitson 这个专卖店大受欢迎，而这个专卖店正是帕丽斯•希尔顿等小报热衷追捧的明星们经常光顾的地方。这些服装上印着杰梅恩的超酷外形，其中一款售价 98 美元的连帽衫上面有他跳舞的图案，背上还写着"没钱，也没烦恼"。Kitson 专卖店在罗伯逊大街上开了三家分店，在其中最大的一家店里，印有杰梅恩肖像的衬衫与售价 290 美元的"辣妹"牛仔裤和 50 美元的婴儿鞋摆放在一起。那些鞋子是由明星吉恩·斯坦芬尼设计的。

"疯狂罗伯逊"这个商标的所有人生长于比弗利山，他在 MySpace 上为杰梅恩建了网页。该网站同时还在为这个品牌和他的同名夜总会做广告。在取得杰梅恩同意之前，几位年轻的创业家花了几个月的时间试图与杰梅恩拉上关系，最后终于打动了他。他现在的名字已经改为约翰·杰米恩了。小伙子们还向杰米恩征询对设计的意见，并请摄影师给他拍照做宣传。

《华尔街报》刊登的合同复印件显示，杰米恩在今年 5 月同意提取服装销售净利润的 5%。他签署了这项合同，但没有向律师和家人透露详情。该品牌服装的创建人特迪·赫什么说，"迄今为止，他一直拒绝接受太多现金，但更愿意接受食品、饮料和纸张。"他也不喜欢在自己的日常生活中牵扯到金钱。"赫什是杰米恩的经纪人及未来规划经理。

赫什表示，杰米恩已经获得了几笔小额报酬，虽然公司到目前为止"并没有赚多少钱"。他还说"我们自己也没有得到什么。"

对于杰米恩的姐姐贝弗莉来说，杰米恩落入无家可归的境地是一个沉痛的话题。这次的服装生意也是如此。她认为"疯狂罗伯逊"的创建人是在利用弟弟的境况炒作他们的品牌。"我想这些年轻人看到了机会就加以利用，"她说，"他们的做法让我不太高兴。"

贝弗莉的家离杰米恩晚上过夜的小巷不远。她说，弟弟有某种精神分裂症。尽管他会爆发间歇性的诅咒和叫嚷，但他拒绝接受药物治疗。64 岁的贝弗莉说，七十年代的后几年，杰米恩的病情开始恶化，从此之后，"我就管不住他了"。贝弗莉在甲骨文公司设备管理部门工作。

八十年代后几年，贝弗莉曾在一个法庭程序中作证，希望迫使弟弟接受帮助。但心理测试的结果显示，杰米恩"头脑清楚，待人和蔼"。为给弟弟提供栖身之地和医学治疗，她曾无数次地努力。现在，她每周会看望他两次，给他带些食物。她还为弟弟交手机费，并代他收社会保障核对表。

将杰米恩包装成前卫人士的事是在无家可归现象日益引起社会关注的背景下产生的。据称，纪录片《游民争斗》已卖出了 30 多万张 DVD，该片讲述的是街头流浪者之间的事。另一部英国电视连续剧《暴富和赤贫》今年也轰动一时，它讲述了装扮成街头乞丐的伦敦百万富翁的生活。

在美国，越来越多的流浪者通过互联网引起了公众的关注。YouTube 上有 17，500 多部视频节目带有"无家可归"一词。得克萨斯州奥斯汀的一位街头流浪汉莱斯利·科恩曾两次竞选市长，他在 MySpace 上拥有 10，755 个"朋友"。在波士顿，无家可归的哈罗德·麦迪逊因有关他的网络视频及一个为他建的网站而声名大振。

杰米恩在汉考克长大，那是洛杉矶的一个有名的老社区，有不少洛杉矶最富有的人家也住在那里。杰米恩的父亲在洛杉矶管理着一家雪佛兰汽车大型专卖店。

杰米恩高中时代是个体育明星，曾被堪萨斯皇家棒球队选中，参加 1969 年的美国职业棒球联盟赛。后来他进入佩珀代因大学，作为洛杉矶 Dodger 队队员参加了在华盛顿举行的一场小型联盟赛。（根据美国棒球研究协会的记录，在 63 场比赛中，他只有 205 次击球，犯规 12 次。）

约耳·罗伯茨是"资助无家可归者"组织的主席，该机构为洛杉矶的街头游民提供住处。在他看来，给杰米恩树立品牌就好比"在伊拉克难民逃离战争后，再给他们设计一块好看的遮羞布。"

对于贝弗莉对弟弟的担忧，赫什和杰米恩品牌另一位创立人维克·阿克曼很在意。不过他们表示，杰米恩"特别关照"他们不要和他姐姐提及该品牌服装以及合同。他们把杰米恩当成"生意伙伴"，并表示他们确信杰米恩很清楚自己的形象是怎样被使用的。

"他对每件事情都了如指掌，"阿克曼说。他同时指出杰米恩还否决了一组宣传照片，因为他不喜欢照片上的行头，认为自己"看上去有点臃肿"。

在跟杰米恩交谈时，他语调柔和，表达简短清晰，其间也穿插着较长的、不那么连贯的评论。法庭记录显示，从1986年以来，他因闯红灯和乱穿马路等行为被多次拘留。目前，他一般都在罗伯逊大街附近溜冰或跳街舞，而过去他总是在比弗利山和西洛杉矶一带游逛，还常常带着内置扬声器，伴随刺耳的音乐舞动。"他一直是个与众不同的舞者，"杰米恩的高中同学吉姆·霍恩说。

除了姐姐，杰米恩还经常与基尼·柏林格联络。柏林格是位64岁的老太太，曾在罗伯逊大街开过古玩店，那时两人就成了朋友。老太太如今住在马里兰，过去曾为杰米恩付过汽车旅馆的住宿费和法式蛋糕店 Michel Richard 每月的咖啡账单。"他想出名，但他不会接受金钱，"柏林格说。

不久前的一个下午，照例系着黑色绑腿、戴着他那标志性帽盔的杰米恩表示，他是"疯狂罗伯逊"品牌的"推动者"，他希望该品牌能进军音乐和影视领域。他是行销独行侠，在罗伯逊大街两旁的墙壁上张贴公司的标识及自己的画像。

在 Kitson 专卖店以及公司的网站上，第一批约 35 件"疯狂罗伯逊"牌女式服装在三天内销售一空。店主弗拉舍·罗斯表示，他们立即又订购了约 90 件。他说，许多网上客户不在洛杉矶，估计也不太了解杰米恩。该品牌也许能吸引其他地方的顾客，大概因为它的名字中有罗伯逊三个字吧，就好像罗迪欧大道总是与高档购物联系在一起一样。

赫什说，Kitson 的成功已经引起了其他零售商的兴趣。他称杰米恩是"我们的迈克尔·乔丹，他正在为"疯狂罗伯逊"的名字和标识申请商标注册。

不过，贝弗莉却不希望这样。"我不想看到弟弟受到伤害，"她说。"他们在利用那些非常容易受伤害、愿意相信他人的人。"

❧单词注释❧

fixture ['fikstʃə] *n.* 固定装置，配件，设备

approval [ə'pru:vəl] *n.* 批准；认可

arrangement [ə'reindʒmənt] *n.* 安排；准备工作

select [si'lekt] *v.* 选择，挑选，选拔

plastering ['plɑ:stəriŋ] *n.* 涂灰泥；上膏药

glamorous ['glæmərəs] *adj.* 富有魅力的；迷人的

❧实用句型 & 词组❧

The swimming pool is available only in summer. (可利用的)

World trade is showing signs of revival. (征兆；前兆)

He went to work despite his illness. (不管，尽管)

❧翻译行不行❧

毫无疑问，好莱坞是引领时尚潮流的中心。

_____

在波士顿，无家可归的哈罗德·麦迪逊因有关他的网络视频及一个为他
建的网站而声名大振。

_____

在跟杰米恩交谈时，他语调柔和，表达简短清晰，其间也穿插着较长的、
不那么连贯的评论。

_____

I Am Still The Greatest

拳王阿里

I have always believed in myself, even as a young child growing up in Louisville, Ky. My parents instilled a sense of pride and confidence in me, and taught me and my brother that we could be the best at anything. I must have believed them, because I remember being the neighborhood marble champion and challenging my neighborhood buddies to see who could jump the tallest hedges or run a foot race the length of the block. Of course I knew when I made the **challenge** that I would win. I never even thought of losing.

In high school, I boasted weekly — if not daily — that one day I was going to be the heavyweight champion of the world. As part of my boxing training, I would run down Fourth Street in downtown Louisville, darting in and out of local shops, taking just enough time to tell them I was training for the Olympics and I was going to win a gold medal. And when I came back home, I was going to turn pro and become the world heavyweight champion in boxing. I never thought of the possibility of failing — only of the fame and glory I was going to get when I won. I could see it. I could almost feel it. *When I proclaimed that I was the "Greatest of All Time," I believed in myself. And I still do.*

Throughout my entire boxing career, my belief in my abilities triumphed over the skill of an opponent. My will was stronger than their skills. What I didn't know was that my will would be tested even more when I retired.

In 1984, I was **conclusively** diagnosed with Parkinson's disease. Since that diagnosis, my symptoms have increased and my ability to speak in audible tones has diminished. If there was anything that would strike at the core of my confidence in myself, it would be this insidious disease. *But my "confidence and will to continue to live life as I choose won't be compromised.*

Early in 1996, I was asked to light the caldron at the Summer Olympic Games in Atlanta. Of course my immediate answer was yes. I never even thought of having Parkinson's or what physical challenges that would present for me.

When the moment came for me to walk out on the 140-foot-high scaffolding and take the torch from Janet Evans, I realized I had the eyes of the world on me. I also realized that as I held the Olympic torch high above my head, my tremors had taken over. Just at that moment, I heard a rumble in the stadium that became a pounding roar and then turned into a deafening applause. I was reminded of my 1960 Olympic experience in Rome, when I won the gold medal. Those 36 years between Rome and Atlanta flashed before me, and I realized that I had come full circle.

Nothing in life has defeated me. I am still the "Greatest." This I believe.

　　我出生在肯塔基州的路易斯维尔，从小就对自己的力量非常有自信。我的父母将自豪感与自信心灌输给了我，他们告诉我和弟弟在任何事情上都要相信自己能够做得最好。我对父母的教诲深信不疑，因为我仍然记得当初我是邻里小朋友中的弹子球冠军。我还记得我向邻居的男孩们挑战，看谁跳过的篱笆更高，或与他们比赛看谁先跑到街区那头。当然，向他们发起挑战时我知道自己会赢——我甚至连想都没想过自己会输。

　　上中学时，我每周都会夸口说——如果算不上天天都说的话——自己有一天将会成为世界重量级拳王。作为拳击训练的一部分，我顺着路易斯维尔商业区的第四大街跑，在当地的商店间来回穿梭，告诉他们我正在为参加奥运会做准备，我要夺冠，说完就走了。而回到家中我要进行职业训练，朝"重量级拳王"迈进。我从未想过我可能会失败——而是想着胜利后的名誉与荣耀。我能看到它。我几乎可以感觉到它。在我宣布自己"永远是最伟大"的拳手时，我相信自己的力量。如今我依然相信。

　　纵观我的拳击生涯，我的自信令我将对手踩在脚下。我胜利的意愿比他们的技术更强。令我没有想到的是，我的这种意愿在我退役后还要接受多次检验。

　　1984 年，我被确诊为帕金森氏病。自确诊之后，我的症状就越来越严重了，我讲话的声音越来越小。如果说有什么事情从根本上挫败了我的信心的话，那就是这种隐伏性的疾病了。但是，我继续按自己选择的道路生活下去的信心和意愿是不会妥协的。

1996 年初，我被邀请在乔治亚州亚特兰大举行的夏季奥运会上点燃主火炬。我毫不犹豫就答应了，根本没有想到我患有帕金森氏病，也没考虑过这所带来的生理挑战。

我从 140 英尺高的架台上走出来，从珍妮特·埃文斯手中接过火炬的那一刻，我意识到全世界的目光此刻都聚集在我的身上。当我将奥运火炬高高举过头顶时，我又意识到全世界的目光都转移到了我震颤着的身体上。就在那一刻，体育馆内响起一阵隆隆声，这隆隆声随后变成一阵轰鸣的叫喊声，最后变成一片震耳欲聋的掌声。这让我想起了 1960 年罗马奥运会，我夺冠时的情景。从罗马到亚特兰大，这 36 年在我眼前一闪而过，我发现我绕了一圈后又回到了这里。

生命中的任何东西都击败不了我。我依旧是"最伟大的"。

❧单词注释❧

challenge ['tʃælindʒ] *n.* 挑战；邀请比赛

proclaim [prə'kleim] *v.* 宣告；公布；声明

conclusively [kən'klu:sivli] *adv.* 决定性地；确定地

flash [flæʃ] *v.* 使闪光；使闪烁

❧实用句型 & 词组❧

We believe in him. (信任)

It's suddenly come back to him where he saw her last. (记起)

The men in this factory walked out yesterday. (罢工)

❧翻译行不行❧

在我宣布自己"永远是最伟大"的拳手时，我相信自己的力量。如今我依然相信。

_____

但是，我继续按自己选择的道路生活下去的信心和意愿是不会妥协的。

_____

生命中的任何东西都击败不了我。我依旧是"最伟大的"。

_____

勇闯天涯
Globe trekker

Top 5 Travel Myths

旅行管家的叮咛

Planning on a trip abroad? Perhaps your summer holiday? Take note of Olivia Sterns'Top 5 Travel Myths. Here they are in bold, and my **comments** to each.

Myth No. 1: Change Money At Home

Olivia says that carrying a large amount of cash makes you vulnerable to pickpockets. Agree. She says it's better to rely on your credit cards. Er, I would say it depends. In a lot of places in Asia, ATM machines are hard to come by and may not accept all ATM cards. In some resorts and hotels in Asia, credit cards are also not accepted. *The exchange rate may also be far worse, depending on the location.* Unless you're staying in a posh destination, never assume that e-transaction will work. Do your research before departure and prepare accordingly.

Myth No. 2: Deals on Last-Minute Booking

Last minutes deals are indeed becoming more and more rare. Better to watch out for sales and promotions (which regularly comes up anyway) to save on **airfares** and hotel bookings.

Myth No. 3: Locals Are Experts

Absolutely not. In fact, in a lot of cases, locals are foreigners to their own territory. In fact, if you're heading off the beaten track, locals can't even understand why, out of all the possible places in the world, you would be interested in their **locality**.

Myth No. 4: You Get What You Pay For

No, particularly in Asia. There are really good deals to be had, some worth far more than you have paid. And vice versa: some expensive digs just aren't worth the top dollar they ask for. Do your research, and look for online reviews.

Myth No. 5: Buy Extras Ahead

When buying packages, you will always be lured into getting a "package", agents telling you it will come out cheaper that way. But, sometimes it pays to be **prudent**.

正在规划你的出国旅游吗？还是正在筹划你的暑假？来关注一下奥利维亚·斯特恩的《旅行五大不得不说的事》吧。看见下面的粗体字了吗？同时也一并附上我的评论。

不得不说之一：在家换好钱

奥利维亚说随身携带巨款的你特别容易引起小偷的注意。我个人完全赞同。她说最好是用信用卡。我个人认为这是因地而异的。在亚洲的很多地方，自动取款机的分布点并不是很多，而且这些自动取款机也不一定能识别所有的卡。在亚洲的一些旅游胜地和酒店，是不能用信用卡的。而由于地区的不同，兑换率也不同，这是个令人头疼的问题。除非你的目的地很现代，很繁华，否则永远不要期望那里的网上交易平台会良好地运转。在出发之前一定要做足相应的准备。

不得不说之二：坚持到最后一秒再预定

在最后一秒预定这个方法现在其实已经越来越少了。为了节省机票费和住宿费，最好时刻关注那些打折或让利信息（基本上是有一定规律可循的）。

不得不说之三：当地人才是真正的专家

这是完全错误的。事实上，在很多情况下，在自己的地盘上，本地人才是真正的外国人。当你被一件对于当地人来说极其平常的事所阻挠时，当地人甚至不明白这个世界上有那么多可以去的地方，为什么你偏偏对他们的地方有兴趣。

不得不说之四：付了钱，你就是老大

这是个错误的想法，尤其是在亚洲。有时的确是物有所值，可能还会物超所值，但反之也亦然。有些贵的离谱的东西并不一定值那个价。研究一下，并且上网查查。

不得不说之五：事先用完你的额度。

当你拎着大包小包时，你很有可能会被说服去买更多的东西。经销商们会告诉你怎么买就可以获得更多的实惠。但是，你买东西的时候最好还是要谨慎些。

旅游中的小学问

• 旅游时带着大围巾，天气突然变冷时，可作无扣女士上衣穿。带小孩游览遇雨，用塑料袋剪成斗篷很方便。

• 在无法洗淋浴时，可用大塑料袋装上水，吊起即成简易淋浴设备。

• 洗后的衬衣想马上穿，可把湿衣放入大塑料袋，向袋内吹热风，衣服很快就干了。

➤单词注释➤

comment ['kɔment] *n.* 注释，评注

location [ləu'keiʃən] *n.* 位置；场所，所在地

airfare ['eəfeə(r)] *n.* 飞机票价

locality [ləu'kæliti] *n.* 地区；场所，现场

prudent ['pru:dənt] *adj.* 审慎的，小心的

➤实用句型 & 词组➤

I'd like to exchange some pounds for dollars. （交换；调换）

The park is becoming more and more beautiful. （越来越）

She is looking for her lost child. （寻找）

➤翻译行不行➤

奥利维亚说随身携带巨款的你特别容易引起小偷的注意，我个人完全赞同。

_____

而由于地区的不同，兑换率也不同，这是个令人头疼的问题。

_____

事实上，在很多情况下，在自己的地盘上，本地人才是真正的外国人。

_____

Conjuring with Grapes

香槟是怎样"炼"成的

It is a tribute to the stimulating **qualities** of really good champagne that by 2:30 we were not only awake, but clearheaded enough to look forward to the afternoon and our studies of the grape's progress, from bunches to bottles.

We began in the white-grape country of the Cotes des Blancs. The vines, which for long periods of the year are empty except for those few slow-moving and patient figures who check to see how nature is getting on, were bristling with people, the narrow green corridors crowded with their autumn population of pickers. It was fine weather for the vendange, mild and dry, and the frosts of late spring had caused less havoc than predicted. This would be a good, plentiful year.

The baskets of grapes were passed up to collection points at the end of the vines and ferried by truck or tractor to the village of Cramant, and the waiting pressoirs. These presses, vast round wooden instruments of torture with slatted sides, are big enough to take tons of grapes at a single gulp. From above, very, very slowly, a giant wooden grill descends on them, bursts them, and crushes them. The glorious juice runs off into subterranean vats.

Three times the grapes are subjected to this remorseless squeeze. Once, to extract the best of the juice, the tête de cuvee ;a second time, for juice that can be used for blending ; and finally, for the remains that will be distilled to make the local eau de vie, the marc de Champagne which they say grows hairs on your chest. Not a drop is wasted, and it is extraordinary to think that a single batch of grapes can be turned into two such different drinks, one delicate and light, the other—well, I happen to like marc, but you could never accuse it of being delicate.

We followed the route of the juice back to the fermentation casks in Epernay, and here I should offer a word of warning. If anyone should ever suggest that you **inhale** the bouquet of champagne in its formative period, decline politely if you value your sinuses. I made the mistake of leaning over an open cask to take a connoisseur's sniff, and very nearly fell backward off the platform to the floor ten feet below. It felt like a noseful of needles. With head swimming and eyes watering, I asked to be led away to a less volatile part of the production line, and we left the casks for an expedition into the bowels of the earth.

Beneath the two famous towns of Reims and Epernay are literally miles of cellars and passageways, some of them three or four stories deep, all of them filled with champagne. In these cool, dim caverns the temperature never varies, and the bottles can doze in perfect conditions, mountain after dark green mountain of them, a champagne lover's foretaste of paradise.

We were in the Perrier-Jouet caves, not enormous by

Champagne standards, but sufficiently big to lose yourself in quite easily. (And very enjoyably, as you would be lost in the middle of twelve million bottles.) The oldest caves, those immediately under the Perrier–Jouet offices, had been hacked out of the chalky earth by hand, and you can see the scars, made by picks and now blackened with age, in the rough arches that lead from one cave to the next. Onward and downward we went, until we came to the angular ranks of tent–shaped wooden racks, each of them sprouting dozens of bottles.

The racks, as tall as a man, were invented in the nineteenth century to solve the problem of the sediment that forms in the bottle as a result of fermentation. The bottles are stuck, neck first, into oval holes set at a steep angle that allows the sediment to slide up to the cork. To make sure this happens completely and evenly, the process needs a little assistance from time to time. The bottles have to be lifted gently, given a slight clockwise turn, and replaced. This is remuage, and despite experimenting with ingenious mechanical methods, progress has yet to find a totally satisfactory replacement for the human hand. Cold and lonely work it must be, too, but an experienced remueur can twist as many as 3,000 bottles an hour.

After remuage comes déorgement. (You'll have to forgive the French words, but their English equivalents don't sound nearly elegant enough to describe the making of champagne.) The neck of the bottle is frozen so that the sediment, trapped in ice, can be removed. The bottle is topped up, recorked, labeled, et voilà! What started as grapes in a **muddy** field has been turned into the most famous drink in the world.

Should you drink it immediately, or lay it down for a year

or two? Or even longer, if it's a vintage champagne? Experts disagree, as experts tend to do, and there are those who say that champagne kept too long will lose its sparkle and character, and become a flat shadow of its former self. *It depends, of course, on the quality of the wine, and I can personally vouch for the benefits of age that we enjoyed on our last night.*

We had been invited to dinner at the hotel particulier of Mumm in Reims. There was our old friend, the Man with the Magnum, and as the courses came and went so did the '85 Cordon Rouge and the '85 Grand Cordon Rose. For the finale, another magnum, this time unlabeled, was nursed to the table as carefully as though it were an extremely rich old aunt from whom one was hoping to inherit. I looked at the menu and saw that it was simply noted as a Very Old Vintage.

I held my glass up to the light and watched the whispers of tiny bubbles rising from the bottom. Whatever else the years had done, they hadn't subdued the sparkle. They had, however, given the wine a very slightly toasted bouquet, the pain grillé nose of a truly **venerable** champagne. It tasted rich and delicate and dry, and it was thirty years old. *There and then, I made up my mind never to drink cheap champagne again. Life is too short.*

真正的好香槟具有提神醒脑的功效。这是香槟酒上乘品质的最好证明。你看，直到下午两点半，我们不仅人是醒着的，

而且头脑还相当清醒，正好可以迎接下午的功课，去研究葡萄由一串串变成一瓶瓶的演进过程。

我们从白丘的白葡萄园开始。这片葡萄园一年中有很长一段时期，都是杳无人烟，只有寥寥数个移动缓慢、吃苦耐劳的人影，在田间查看葡萄的生长情况。但现在是农忙时节，园中狭长的绿色走廊，挤满了秋收的采摘者。这时正是采收葡萄的好天气，暖和又干爽。而晚春的霜降带来的损害也比预期要少。今年将是个很好的丰收年。

人们把一篮又一篮的葡萄送到了田尾的收集点，再用卡车或拖拉机运到克拉蒙村的玛姆酒庄。那里的榨酒机早已恭候多时了。这些用来折磨葡萄的榨汁机是一种木制的、巨大的圆形设备，侧边都是百叶板。这巨无霸一口足以吞下几吨葡萄。然后，一块巨大的木制压板自上而下，以非常非常慢的速度落下，压在葡萄上，将它们压破，挤榨出汁，之后源源流入地下的大桶里。

葡萄遭受这样无情的压榨，前后共需三次。第一次榨出的是最上等的葡萄汁，叫作"葡萄酒酒头"；第二次榨的汁，则用在混成酒上；最后一次压榨的残汁，蒸馏以后用来酿成当地人喝的"白兰地"，也就是他们说的、会促使你胸部长毛的"渣酿香槟"。一滴也不浪费，太不可思议了。同一批葡萄居然能变出两种差别这么大的酒。一种雅致、清淡；另一种呢——嗯，我刚好喜欢渣酿酒，但你恐怕永远不会用"雅致"一词来形容它。

我们沿着葡萄汁走过的路线来到了发酵桶这边。此时，我要提醒大家的是，万一有人建议你吸一口发酵期的香槟气味，请你婉言谢绝。我就犯了这个错误，倾身靠向一只敞开的酒桶，想以鉴赏家的派头嗅上一嗅，结果我差点从离地十英尺高的平台上跌下来。当时我只觉得鼻子像是针扎一样难受。我感到一阵子头晕目眩，恳请挪到生产线上气味不那么厚重的地方休养生息。接着，我们便弃此酒桶，转往地球内部探险去也。

在莱姆斯和艾柏内这两座名城的地底下，其实有长达数英里的地窖和通道，有的深达三四层楼。里面全都塞满了香槟。地窖凉爽、幽暗，温度始终保持恒定。所以，一瓶瓶的葡萄酒便能在这完美的储存条件下大睡其觉。它们仿佛墨绿色的山峦，重重叠叠，果真是香槟爱好者的极乐世界。

我们来到佩利耶•珠玉的地窖。按照香槟区的标准，这地窖算不上大，但也大到足以让你一不留神就会迷失在里面。（迷失在 1200 万瓶窖藏葡萄酒里，也未尝不是一件令人愉快的事情。）其中最古老的地窖，就在佩利耶•珠玉的办事处的正下方，是由人工从白垩土质地面向下开凿出来的，你现在还能看得见挖凿的痕迹，留存在连接一间间地窖的、粗糙的拱门上，并因岁月积淀而变得发黑。随后，我们一路走下来，行至深处，来到一排排像帐篷一样、呈锐角排列的木制搁物架前。只见每个架子里都是酒瓶林立。

这些木架子被称作"人字型酒架"，是在 19 世纪时发明出来的，为的是解决香槟酒因发酵而在瓶内形成沉淀的问题。这些瓶子倒竖着，插在架子的椭圆形洞内，呈陡斜的角度，以便沉淀物能慢慢滑落到瓶塞处。为了确保沉淀物能完全、均匀地滑落下来，这过程时不时需要人为帮忙一下。举起酒瓶要轻柔，再按顺时针方向稍微转动一下，然后放回原处。这个过程叫"转瓶"。虽然也尝试过一些借助智能机器的方法，但是要找到完全令人满意、可以取代人类双手的替代物，还有待继续努力。这想必是一个冰冷又寂寥的工作，但是，一个熟练的转瓶工人，1小时可以处理多达 3，000 瓶的酒。

转瓶工序完成之后，接下来就是"除渣"了，就是将酒瓶颈部冷冻起来，以便取出冻结在冰里面的沉淀物。然后，加满酒瓶里的酒，重新塞上软木塞，贴上标签，就此大功告成！出自泥泞田野的葡萄一下子脱胎换骨，变成琼浆玉液了。

你是立马喝上一口呢，还是存放个一年两年，甚至更久？（如果这是好年份的香槟的话。）专家们对此也意见不一，他们总是这样。有些人说香槟如果存放太久不喝，会失去它的泡沫和风味，变得像酿制之前一样平淡。当然这要看酒的品质如何了。而我个人是敢担保经年陈酿的好处的，就像我们在最后一晚享用的那瓶酒一样。

我们受邀到莱姆斯城的玛姆特色饭庄进晚餐。席间有我们的老友，就是捧着大酒瓶的那位仁兄。一道道菜肴送上、撤下，标有 1985 年份的红绶带和大绶带玫瑰红香槟也随之进进出出。最后压轴的是一瓶未贴标签的美酒——仿佛是一位极其富有的老妇人，而我们要从她那儿继承点什么似的，被小心翼翼地呈上了桌面。我瞧了一眼菜单，上面只是简单的注明是陈年老酒。

我举起酒杯迎向灯光，端详细小的泡沫由杯底升腾时的私语。不管岁月用了些什么手法，都不曾制伏这些泡沫。不过，时光倒是为这美酒添加了一缕幽淡的烤面包的香气。这是真正年份久远的香槟美酒才会散发出来的气味，入口馥郁、雅致、清淡，酒龄 30 岁。此时此刻，我下定决心永远不再喝一口廉价的香槟。人生苦短啊！

☙单词注释❧

quality ['kwɔliti] *n.* 质，质量

inhale [in'heil] *v.* 吸入

muddy ['mʌdi] *adj.* 多烂泥的；泥泞的

venerable ['venərəbl] *adj.* 令人肃然起敬的；可尊敬的

☙实用句型 & 词组❧

They are looking forward to her visit.（盼望）

Sam is as rich as Alexander.（同样地）

He noted the importance of the problem in his lecture.（提到，指明）

☙翻译行不行❧

我们从白丘的白葡萄园开始。

_____

当然这要看酒的品质如何了。而我个人是敢担保经年陈酿的好处的，就像我们在最后一晚享用的那瓶酒一样。

_____

此时此刻，我下定决心永远不再喝一口廉价的香槟。人生苦短啊！

_____

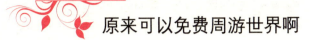

Travel the World for Free
原来可以免费周游世界啊

World travel is cheap and easy. In fact, with a little practice and **effort**, you can travel the world for free.

1. Embrace the Simple Joy of Travel

Travel frees you from the grind of daily routine. You will **explore** new places, meet new people, try new foods and learn things about the world — and yourself — that you never imagined were possible. The joy of new experience is the most wonderful thing about travel — and new experiences are free. Walk the streets of a city. Stop and chat with a local. People watch in a public park. Climb to the top of a hill and watch the sun set over the ocean.

2.Keep Your Needs To A Minimum

People need fresh air, healthy food, clean water, exercise, creative stimulation, companionship, self-esteem and a safe place to sleep.

All of these things are simple to obtain. Most of them are free. For fresh air, go outside. For exercise, take a walk. For creative stimulation, go somewhere new. For companionship, make a friend. For self—esteem, turn off your TV, breathe deep and open your spirit to the basic goodness of the world.

Things like food and shelter are much cheaper once you get outside the United States. See 5 below for ways to obtain food and **shelter** for free.

3. Go Slow

If you live in New York and want to take a 2 week vacation to Africa, it will be very difficult (though not impossible, see number eight) to travel for free.

Indeed, as long as you believe that time is money, you will spend money all the time. Time is not money. Time is free. You have all the time in the world.

Instead of buying a plane ticket, catch a ride out West, or remodel an old sailboat, or just hop on your bike and ride away from town. The slower you travel, the less money you will spend.

4. Leave Your Possessions and Obsessions Behind

When you travel, you don't need to pay rent. You don't need a car. You don't need an oven, a washer—dryer, electricity, Cable TV, a gym membership, a sofa and loveseat or a closet full of clothes. You don't need a suit and tie to wear to your job because you don't need a job. You don't need to worry about paying the bills, because there are no bills to pay.

You are free.

5. Trust People and you will Receive Free Food and Lodging

Many people are willing to open their homes to travelers, and they will give you a free meal, too.

CouchSurfing and WWOOF are two phenomenal online networks that help travelers connect with local hosts. CouchSurfing members are willing to give travelers a place to sleep for a night or two. WWOOF **connects** travelers with organic farmers who want to trade room and board for an extra hand.

6. Learn a Useful Craft or Skill

If you have a skill, such as cooking, animal husbandry, massage, musical ability or basic carpentry, you can barter for free food and **accommodation** as you travel.

Universally appreciated skills like cooking are best, though niche skills that are in high demand, like website design, are also useful. Native English speakers can often travel the world for free by teaching language classes in each destination they visit.

The slower you travel, the easier it will be to work out a mutually beneficial arrangement with a local community or host.

7. Get Out of the City

Although it's possible to travel for free in a big city, it's damn difficult.

Go to the country, where people are more relaxed, food is plentiful and there's ample room for one traveler to lay out her sleeping bag under the stars.

8. Find A Job You Love That Entails Travel

If you need an income in order to pay off loans or support a child, find a job that calls for extensive travel. There are millions of jobs **available** in the global economy that demand travel.

Of course, some jobs are easier to love than others, and much work that involves travel also involves the destruction of local ecosystems and traditional ways of life. Avoid unethical work if at all possible —it is bad for your health and worse for your soul.

9.Embrace Serendipity

Traveling the world for free requires a blend of advance planning and the willingness to seize opportunities and go with the flow.

Does your new CouchSurfing friend want company for a drive across the country? Grab your pack and ride along! Does an organic farm in Thailand need a farm sitter for the **rainy** season? Get in touch with Christian Shearer!

As Kurt Vonnegut wrote, "Peculiar travel suggestions are dancing lessons from God."

Go Dancing.

环球旅行是一项既省钱又简单的事情。实际上，只需一点点行动和努力，你就可以免费环游世界。在这里，我和大家一起来分享一下免费旅游的心得。

1. 把旅行搞得轻松愉快点

旅游把你从繁琐的日常工作中解脱了出来。你可以探索新的地方，结交新的朋友，尝试没有吃过的食物，了解这个世界的新事物，甚至重新审视自我。这些都是你从未想过的。体验新鲜算是旅游的最大乐趣了。徜徉在一座陌生城市的街道上，走走停停，和当地的人们聊聊天，在公园里看人们行走在景色中，登高远眺，去看海上日出，这一切都是新鲜的，而且是免费的。

2. 缩减你的需求

人需要的是什么呢？是新鲜的空气，健康的食物，洁净的饮用水，人类还需要运动，灵感，伴侣，自我，以及一个安全的休憩之地。

所有这些事情都很容易实现，而是它们中的大部分还都是免费的。新鲜的空气和运动只需外出散散步就可以获得，灵感的激发到一个新的地方自会出现。交朋友自会获得伴侣，关掉电视深呼吸，打开心灵面对世上的真善美，就会找到真正的自我了。

如果你去除美国之外的地方旅游，食物和住宿立刻就便宜了不少，下面第 5 条会告诉你如何获得免费的食宿。

3. 放慢行走的脚步

如果你住在纽约，想用两周的假期到非洲旅游，要想免费就实在不是件易事了（尽管不是完全不可能，请看第 8 条）。

实际上，只要你相信时间就是金钱，那么你就一直在花钱。时间并不是金钱，时间是免费的，你拥有世界上的一切时间。

别买机票，而是骑马穿越西部；或者改造一条旧船，或者干脆骑自行车外出远行。你走的越慢，花的钱也就越少。

4. 御下一切负担

旅游的时候，你不需要付房租，汽车、微波炉、洗衣机、电、有线电视、健身会员卡、沙发和装满衣服的衣柜，这些你通通不需要。你也不必再西装革履，因为你已经不再工作了。你也不必担心要花钱，因为根本没有需要花钱的地方。

一切都是自由而免费的。

5. 相信别人，你会得到免费的食宿

很多人愿意打开家门迎接旅游的朋友们，他们还会为你提供免费的午餐。

CouchSurfing 和 WWOOF 是两个热门的网站，驴友可以通过它联系到当地的接待家庭。CouchSurfing 的用户都愿意为旅行者提供一个可以睡一两天的住处。WWOOF 会联系驴友，当地的有机农场的农民愿意以超低价把房子租给你。

6. 掌握一种有用的技能

如果你有一技之长，比如烹饪、饲养动物，按摩，音乐才能或一些基本的木工活,你就可以拿这些来换免费的食物和住处了。

在大家普遍公认的技能里，烹饪是最受欢迎的。尽管一些像网页设计这样的高级技能也很有用。母语是英语的旅行者可以通过教英语来获得免费的旅游机会。

你走的越慢，越容易找到可以和当地社会或主人互利互益的方法。

7. 到郊外去

尽管你也可以在一座大城市免费旅行，但是这相对要困

难些。

到郊外去，那里的人们过着轻松的生活，有充足的食物和宽敞的房间供旅行者享用，你甚至可以在外面露宿。

8. 找份需要旅行的工作

如果你需要一笔收入来还贷款或养孩子，那就找份需要经常出差的工作吧，有好多工作需要环球旅行。

当然，有些工作会让你更容易爱上它，当然那些包括旅游的工作也同样带来了当地生态系统的破坏和传统生活方式的改变。尽量避免做那些不道德的工作，它们不利于你的身心健康。

9. 拥抱新发现

免费的环球旅行需要提前计划，以及随遇而安、抓住一切机会的态度。

你在 CouchSurfing 上的新好友是不是想要一个驾车旅行的同伴？背上行囊立即出发吧！泰国有机农场是否需要一个雨季的农场看管员呢？到 Christian Shearer 网站看看去吧！

库尔特·冯内古特写过："独特的旅行建议是上帝给我们的舞蹈课"。

让我们跳起来吧！

❧单词注释❧

effort ['efət] *n.* 努力，尽力

explore [iks'plɔ:] *v.* 探测；探勘

shelter ['ʃeltə] *n.* 遮盖物；躲避处

connect [kə'nekt] *v.* 连接

accommodation [ə,kɔmə'deiʃən] *n.* 适应；调节

available [ə'veiləbl] *adj.* 可用的，在手边的

rainy ['reini] *adj.* 下雨的；多雨的

❧实用句型 & 词组❧

I was tied to my job by a contract. （束缚，约束）

We started early in order to arrive before dark. （为了）

He was suddenly seized with panic. （支配，控制）

❧翻译行不行❧

环球旅行是一项既省钱又简单的事情。

_____

所有这些事情是那么容易实现，而它们中的大部分都是免费的。

_____

如果你需要一笔收入来还贷款或养孩子，那就找份工作来为昂贵的旅行
买单吧。

_____

Top Five Island Destinations

天堂秘境：一生要去的五大岛屿

Chiloé , Chile

The Chiloé archipelago's **pristine** seascape is one reason the islands tied for third place in a new ranking of the world's best kept island destinations — and quite a few that are succumbing to tourism overkill.

Shetland Islands, Scotland, U.K.

A lighthouse by the Eshaness Cliffs together with two other destinations for third place among 111 islands rated on their preservation record and forecast.

As one of the 522 expert judges said in the November/ December 2007 issue of National Geographic Traveler magazine, the islands have "spectacular sea cliffs ;pristine beaches ; fascinating geology ;over a million breeding seabirds ;the highest density of otters in Europe ;regular sightings of killer whales ;and superb displays of rare sub—Arctic flora."

About 130 miles (210 kilometers) north of mainland Scotland, the islands were applauded for the preservation of both heritage and **ecology**, despite nearby oil developments.

"A unique blend of Scotland and Nordic culture," wrote another expert. "Somewhat remote, the Shetlands have protected the environment and continue to attract tourists and maintain other sectors (fishing and oil) in harmony."

Lofoten, Norway

The Lofoten island group — including the town of Reine — tied with two other destinations for third place among 111 islands rated on their record of **sustainable** environmental and cultural practices.

"The weather is often rotten, but the beauty of the sea, rocks, and houses is awe-inspiring," said one of the 522 experts judging the islands.

Like many of the list's top-scoring islands, the Lofoten archipelago in the Norwegian Sea has avoided excessive tourism partly because its nippy climate doesn't draw the beach-party set. Lofoten won praise for its "deep, placid fjords," and "jagged, rocky peaks."

Still, "cruising tourism is a threat," cautioned another expert ranker.

Azores, Portugal

These islands—including Flores—lie about 1,000 miles (1,600 kilometers) west of **continental** Portugal.

The Azores are home to green volcanic mountains and picturesque towns—attributes noted by one of 522 experts who helped judge 111 islands for National Geographic Traveler magazine.

The archipelago was ranked second because the Azore's strong culture and healthy ecosystems are likely to last, especially since the islands' "capricious climate probably impedes the flow of tourists," according to another expert participating in the ranking.

Faroe Islands, Denmark

Part of Denmark, this self-governing North Atlantic archipelago is home to a population one expert called "unified and resolutely Faroese, not Danish."

"Cultural integrity strong," agreed another expert judge, who added caution to the praise, "If the numbers of cruise ships continue to grow rapidly, there may be problems..."

Despite such concern, the Faroe Islands were voted the most "authentic, unspoiled, and likely to remain so" of 111 islands ranked by volunteer expert judges for the November/December 2007 issue of *National Geographic Traveler* magazine.

A cool climate and remote location have kept many tourists away, leaving "lovely, unspoiled islands" that are "a delight to the traveler."

智利 奇洛埃

奇洛埃岛质朴的海景是该岛名列最新榜单"世界保存最完好的岛屿"，并成为该榜单季军的原因之一，而很多岛屿都因为旅游破坏严重而没有入选。

英国苏格兰 设得兰群岛

爱莎奈斯悬崖上的灯塔，与另外两处保存完好的风光，预示着设得兰群岛将在 111 个岛屿中名列三甲。

522 位专家评审中的一位曾在《国家地理旅行者》的 2007 年 11、12 月刊中这样写道：此岛拥有"壮观的海崖；质朴的海滩；迷人的地理景色；上百万只饲养的海鸟；欧洲密度最高的水獭；虎鲸时常出没；亚北极地区罕见的植物群在此华丽地呈现。"

在苏格兰主岛以北约 130 英里（即 210 公里）的地方，一些岛屿因历史遗产及生态景观双双出彩而受到赞赏，尽管其附近在开采油田。

另一个专家写道："这里是苏格兰和北欧文化的独特融合地，尽管有些偏远，设得兰却一直在保护环境和吸引游客方面下大工夫，并维持了其他部分（捕鱼及石油开采），所有这一切在这里得到了和谐共存。"

挪威 罗浮敦岛

包括勒奈城在内的罗浮敦群岛与另外两处景点，凭借其一直以来对环境的保护及文化的实践,在 111 个岛屿中名列三甲。

522 位专家中的一位在评判此群岛时曾这样说:"这里的气候常年恶劣,但是这里的大海、岩石以及房屋,却美丽得令人惊叹。"

与榜单上其他得分较高的岛屿一样,挪威海的罗浮敦群岛因其凛冽的气候不适合海滩晚会,而未造成旅游过度。罗浮敦群岛因其"纵深、平静的海湾"和"起伏、多岩石的山峰"而获此殊荣。

而且另一位曾任军官的专家也曾警告说:"在此乘船旅行可能会遇到危险"。

葡萄牙 亚述尔群岛

包括弗洛里斯岛在内的这些岛屿,位于葡萄牙陆地以西约 1,000 英里处(1,600 公里)。

522 位曾为《国家地理旅行者》对 111 个岛屿进行评判的专家组中的一位如此归结此岛屿的特征:亚述尔岛到处是翠绿的火山,小镇风景如画。

另一位参与此评审的专家说,此群岛名列第二,是因为亚述尔的深厚的文化和健康的生态系统可能会得以继续保持,尤其是该岛屿"多变的天气可能会阻止大批旅行团的到来。"

丹麦 法罗群岛

作为丹麦的一部分,这个自治的北大西洋群岛居住着被一位专家称为"统一且绝对的法罗人,而不是丹麦人"。

另一个专家评审在赞赏之后提出了警告,"这里的文化保持地非常完整,如果游览船只不断增多,就可能会引发问题……"

　　撇开这种担忧，在《国家地理旅行者》的 2007 年 11、12 月刊上，法罗岛被志愿的专家评审票选为这 111 个岛屿中最"可信、完好无损且可能一直保持下去"的岛屿。

　　这里的凉爽气候以及偏远的位置让很多游客无法亲近，反而成为让"游客们十分欢喜"的"孤独、完整的岛屿"。

最大的岛与群岛

　　世界上最大的岛屿是格陵兰岛，面积达 217.56 万平方公里。世界上最大的群岛是马来群岛，由苏门答腊岛、加里曼丹岛、爪哇岛、菲律宾群岛等 2 万多个岛屿组成，沿赤道延伸 6，100 公里，南北最大宽度 3，500 公里，总面积约 243 万平方公里，约占世界岛屿面积的 20%。

❧单词注释❧

pristine [ˈpristain] *adj.* 原始的；清新的

ecology [i(ː)ˈkɔlədʒi] *n.* 生态学；生态，环境

sustainable [səˈsteinəbl] *adj.* 能承受的；能保持的；能维持的

continental [ˌkɔntiˈnentl] *adj.* 洲的；大陆的

caution [ˈkɔːʃən] *n.* 小心，谨慎

location [ləuˈkeiʃən] *n.* 位置；场所，所在地

❧实用句型 & 词组❧

John is likely to be in London this autumn. （很可能的）

We are all partly to blame. （部分地；不完全地）

The fire is going out；will you add some wood? （添加；增加）

❧翻译行不行❧

爱莎奈斯悬崖上的灯塔，与另外两处保存完好的风光，预示着设得兰群岛在 111 个岛屿中名列三甲。

_____

另一位参与此评审的专家说，此群岛名列第二，是因为亚述尔的深厚的文化和健康的生态系统可能会得以继续保持，尤其是该岛屿"多变的天气可能会阻止大批旅行团的到来。"

_____

这里的凉爽气候以及偏远的位置让很多游客无法亲近，反而成为让"游客们十分欢喜"的"孤独、完整的岛屿"。

_____

Dear Old Things
"业余" 古董玩家

It is a tiresome habit of many antique dealers to mark their prices in code. Sometimes it is a straightforward substitution of letters for numerals, so that A equals 1, D equals 4, and so on. More often, the letters are given complicated values that make no sense at all to anyone other than the dealer, and so we find that our chest of drawers is clearly marked "XPT."

What does that mean? Would he accept XOS in cash for a quick sale? Why can't the rascal mark his prices in dollars and cents like they do at Bloomingdale's? What is he playing at?

The game is called "matching the price to the customer." While you have been looking at the chest of drawers, the dealer has been looking at you, and you're both considering the same question—how much?—from different points of view. Depending on how you're dressed, how interested you seem to be in buying, and how interested he is in selling, the price might **fluctuate** significantly. But you're not to know that. It is one of the dealer's little secrets.

Don't let it worry you, because you can play the game, too. Call the man over, and get a price from him. Whatever figure he mentions, brush it aside. No, no, you say. Give me the trade price. (Normally, quite a lot less.)

The dealer will look at you through narrowed eyes. Are you really another dealer, or just a robber in a well-cut suit? You give him a business card and show him your checkbook, and there it is, printed proof: COOPER ANTIQUES, PERIOD FURNITURE, VIEWING BY APPOINTMENT ONLY.

I know a man who has been doing this for years, and he has now completely refurnished his house at special trade prices, even though he's no more a dealer than my butcher's dog is. When I asked him if he thought that this was the kind of sharp **practice** that an unsporting judge might describe as fraudulent misrepresentation, he just grinned. Didn't I know? Most antiques bounce back and forth between dealers for years before they find places in private homes. All he was doing, in his own small way, was helping to speed up the turnover of stock, giving the dealers the money to go out and buy more antiques from other dealers. The way he saw it, he was doing the entire business a service.

Even if you're not prepared to disguise yourself as a gentleman dealer, you must still resist the impulse to pay the asking price. Make an offer, but not before making a few disparaging remarks about rickety legs, dents, scars, and interesting blemishes that have accrued with the passage of centuries. The dealer expects it. In fact, he might be hurt if you didn't point them out, because he may have spent several days in his workshop putting them on.

The process of aging an object or a piece of furniture overnight—or "distressing" it—is an art in itself, and it is miraculous what a talented distresser can do with rusty nails and pumice stone and a mixture of soot and bees-wax. More miraculous still is how three-legged chairs can suddenly sprout a fourth leg, marquetry with a bad case of acne can regain a smooth complexion, and tables originally constructed for midgets can grow to adult height.

Inevitably, some killjoy will try to belittle these marvels of inventive restoration. We all have at least one acquaintance who is a self-appointed expert and whose mission in life is to tell you that you have bought a fake. Shaking his head at your foolishness, he will point out in great detail what you were too dumb to see for yourself. It's not a bad piece, he'll say, but you could hardly call it a genuine antique. But what the hell. Does it matter? If the piece pleases you, if the faking has been done well, who cares? You bought it to live with, not to sell. The antique know-it-all is a pest who should be locked up in the bowels of the Metropolitan Museum to study pre-Columbian bidets.

Occasionally the situation will be reversed and a genuine piece will be treated with as little respect as would a sheet of plywood. I was once in a Manhattan antique shop when a decorator came in with his client. (I knew he was a decorator by the effortless way in which he spent thousands of dollars in the first ten minutes.) He paused in front of a magnificent fifteenth-century oak dining table— absolutely authentic, in wonderful condition, a piece of great **rarity**. He heard the price without flinching. "We'll take it," he said, "but you'll have to cut two feet off the end so that it will fit in the breakfast alcove."

The dealer was in shock. *I don't like to see a man wrestle with his **conscience**, so I didn't wait to see whether he sold the table or whether his principles got the better of him.* Personally, I like antiques to be used rather than worshiped, but I did wonder how the table's maker would have felt about his work being chopped up and put in a breakfast nook.

Over the years I have been attracted to a wide variety of antiques, an admirer of all and an expert on none. I have liked Chippendale chairs, Chinese porcelain, kitchen artifacts, Lalique glass, Georgian commodes—just about everything except art, which is a separate and overpriced world of its own. Unfortunately for my aspirations as a collector, I have realized that nature did not equip me for the task. I can't stand living with objects that I have to tiptoe around and hardly dare to touch. I like to be able to sit on chairs, eat at tables, drink from glasses, and collapse onto beds without feeling that I am committing sacrilege or risking breakage and financial ruin. I now live with furniture and objects that are either virtually indestructible or easily replaceable. Old, perhaps, but sturdy. I avoid fragility.

And there is something else that I avoid and that, if you are only a moderately rich millionaire, you should avoid, too: the chic auction.

The people who go to the big salesrooms, glossy brochures tucked under mink-clad arms, are not like you and me. *They might be upper-crust dealers, professional bidders for foundations, or just grade-A plutocrats, but they have one thing in common: they are loaded.* And when loaded people get together in the overcranked atmosphere of competitive bidding, prices disappear upward within seconds. If you should decide, out of curiosity, to be a spectator at one of these million-dollar orgies, the golden rule is to sit on your hands. One absentminded scratch of your ear might catch the auctioneer's eye and you could find yourself with a twelfth-century bleeding cup and a bill the size of a **mortgage**. You're safer with Art Nouveau coatracks.

　　许多古董商有个讨厌的习惯，喜欢用代码来标价。有时是直接以字母替代数字，如 A 代表 1，D 代表 4，以此类推。更常见的情况是，字母代表的意思曲里拐弯，复杂极了，除了古董商以外，没有人能弄明白。所以，我们才会发现我们看中的五斗柜上，清清楚楚地标了个"XPT"。

　　那是什么意思啊？如果现金结账，迅速成交，他能接受"XOS"吗？这无赖难道不能像曼哈顿的布鲁明黛尔百货公司那样，用元、角、分来标价吗？他到底玩的是什么把戏呢？

　　这游戏叫做"看人出价"。就在你仔细端详那只五斗柜时，古董商也在上上下下打量你，而你们俩都在心里盘算同一个问题——多少钱？只是看法、角度各异罢了。凭你的穿着、你购买欲望的大小、你出手兴趣的高低，价格可以上下大幅波动。但你是不会知晓个中玄机的，这是古董商的一个小秘密。

　　你不用为此烦心，因为你同样可以玩这套把戏。你只管把那男子叫过来，问他价钱。无论他报什么价，都把它晾在一边。不对，不对，你也可以说，给我个行价吧（通常价格会少很多）。

那古董商会眯起眼来打量你。难道你也是个古董商？或只是一个衣冠楚楚的强盗？你递给他一张名片。再给他看你的支票簿，上面清清楚楚地印着几行字："库珀古玩店，老式家具，只限预约看货"。

我认识一个人，他这么做已经有好多年了。虽然他和那个肉贩子养的狗一样，和古董商一点关系都没有，但到现在，他已经靠如此这般的特惠价，把整个家又重新装潢了一遍。有次我问他，用这种不正当的手段找便宜，若碰上个正经八百、光明正大的法官，会不会判你个招摇撞骗罪呢？他只是咧嘴笑了一笑。难道我会不知道吗？大部分的古董要在各家古董商之间来回倒腾好几年，才会找到一户人家好生安顿下来的。他利用这套小把戏所做的一切，无非是为了帮助古董商加快存货周转的速度，好让他们腾出更多的资金，到外面向别的商家买进更多的古董。照他的说法，他这是在造福整个古董业。

即使你并无打算把自己假扮成一个绅士派头十足的古董商，你仍然要抑制住内心的冲动，千万不可乖乖地按对方的出价付钱，一定要还价。但还价前，你一定要对想买的东西贬损一番，比如说，脚站不稳啦，有凹痕，还有刮伤，以及一些因岁月流转而自然产生的斑驳陆离的缺陷。实际上，古董商正等着你这样做呢。你如果挑不出毛病来，他可能还觉得自尊心受到了伤害。因为，那些所谓的缺陷搞不好是他花了好几天的时间，才在作坊里制造出来的呢。

一晚上便让一样东西或是一件家具衰老上几十年、甚至几百年——姑且称之为"折磨"吧，它本身也是一种艺术。正是这些行刑的天才靠着生锈的铁钉、粗粝的浮石，加上煤灰与蜜蜡的混合物，创造了种种神奇。还有更神奇的呢，原来三只脚的椅子会突然长出第四只脚；原来满是青春痘的镶嵌工艺，会重现光滑的面容；原来给侏儒做的矮桌子，会一下子蹿到普通成人的高度。

当然，你不免会碰到个把煞风景的家伙，总想贬低这些变造复古的创举。我们至少认识一个这样的人。他自封为内行。他毕生的使命就是要告诉你，你买到的全是假货。他一边晃着脑袋说你笨，一边事无巨细、不厌其烦地向你指出，你怎么笨到连这一处都没看出来呀。他会说，这物件虽然算不上糟糕，但你不能说它是真古董。但那又有什么关系吗？如果你喜欢这东西，又假得高明，几可乱真，谁管它是真、还是假？更何况你买它是为了在生活里用的，又不是为了去卖。其实，这些无所不知的古董专家都是公害，应该关进大都会博物馆的最里面，让他们去研究前哥伦布时期的澡盆。

偶尔也有乾坤颠倒的情况。一件真品被当作了一张胶合板似的东西而得不到应有的尊重。我有一次在曼哈顿的古董店，碰见了一位室内装饰设计师，带着他的客户来到店中。（我看得出来他是室内设计师。因为一进门，他就在 10 分钟之内轻松花掉了好几千美金。）在一张外表华丽的 15 世纪橡木餐桌（绝对是真品）前面，他停了下来。桌子保存情况也非常好，可算是一件稀世珍宝。他听了价钱后，显出一副毫不畏缩的样子，说："我们要买它，但你必须锯掉它的两只脚，这样它才能被塞进壁龛里当早餐桌用。"

古董商大吃一惊。我不愿看到一个人良心挣扎的样子。所以，我没有留下来看他是卖掉了桌子呢，还是他的原则占了上风。

我喜欢古董能为人所用，而不是当神供起来。但我的确还是想知道，造这张桌子的匠人，若是知道他的作品被截肢，并被塞进某个角落里当了餐桌，他不知该作何感想啊。

多年来，我感兴趣的古董种类繁多。我是什么都爱，但什么都不精。我曾喜欢过18世纪英国齐本德尔式的椅子，中国的瓷器，厨房用品，雕花玻璃和乔治王时代的橱柜——除了艺术作品以外，几乎无所不爱。因为这艺术作品自成一个单独的、定价过高的领域。虽然我渴望成为一名收藏家，但不幸的是，我发现上苍并没有赋予我应有的天资。我忍受不了生活里有什么东西，让我在经过时不得不蹑手蹑脚地绕过去，甚至不敢碰它一下。我喜欢椅子就是给人坐的，桌子就是用来在上面吃东西的，玻璃杯就是可以拿来喝水的，床就是可以往上面砰然倒下的，而无需觉得我是在亵渎宝物，或是冒东西被毁甚至破产的风险。现在我生活里用的家具和物品，要么是坏不了的，要么很容易找到替代品。或许它们很老，但很坚固。我对脆弱可是敬而远之的。

另外还有一件事，我也是敬而远之的。而且，你如果只是个中不溜秋的百万富翁，那你更该对它敬而远之：那就是时髦的拍卖会。

那些身着貂皮大衣，手臂下夹着精装目录走进大拍卖场的人，绝非不入流的、你我可与攀比之辈。他们可能是上流的古董商，也可能是代表基金会的职业投标人，要不就是顶级的富豪，他们共有一个特点：富得流油。一群极其富有的人在一起扎堆，在竞买火暴的气氛里，不出几秒钟就能把价格哄抬到九霄云外。假如你出于好奇，决定当一回看客，出席这种一掷千金、面不改色的狂欢会，那你就应该遵守一条金科玉律：把手搁在屁股底下。也许你的一个不经意的动作，只是抓了一下耳朵，可能就会被眼尖的拍卖师逮个正着。然后，你就会发现有一个 12 世纪的滴血杯和一张数额大如抵押贷款的账单，摆在了你的面前。看来，还是买那种新艺术风格的衣帽架更保险些。

艺术品收藏趋势

专题收藏一直是近年来收藏界的一个方向。比如像邮品、钱币、磁卡、字画、瓷器、玉器、铜器、宝石、名人印章、明清家具、创刊号报纸、门券、烟标、火花、图书、像章、藏书票、根雕、牙雕、请柬等，可谓五花八门、包罗万象。不过，专题收藏可能会更强调珍品化。无论如何，一个收藏者要提高收藏品位和收藏档次，收藏珍品必不可少。但凡有名的收藏者，都有一些经过时间和市场考验的珍品，这已成为收藏界的一种共识。

☙单词注释❧

fluctuate ['flʌktjueit] *v.* 波动，变动；动摇

practice ['præktis] *n.* 实行，实施

rarity ['rɛəriti] *n.* 稀有，罕见

conscience ['kɔnʃəns] *n.* 良心；道义心

mortgage ['mɔːgidʒ] *n.* 抵押

☙实用句型 & 词组❧

There's nobody here other than me. （除了）

This method went out long ago. （过时）

The news of his death was a shock to us. （震惊）

☙翻译行不行❧

你不用为此烦心，因为你同样可以玩这套把戏。

我不愿看到一个人良心挣扎的样子。所以，我没有留下来看他是卖掉了
桌子呢，还是他的原则占了上风。

他们可能是上流的古董商，也可能是代表基金会的职业投标人，要不就
是顶级的富豪，他们共有一个特点：富得流油。

Spotlight on Hawaii
夏威夷印象

*For most of us, Hawaii begins to weave her spell with some little **glimmer** of awareness.* Golden beaches and golden people. Sun, sand, sea, and surf...And somewhere between the blue skies and the palm trees...we're hooked.

The Hawaiian Islands are one of the most beautiful places on earth. The weather is friendly. The **temperature** ranges from 60–90 degrees all year long. It's a little warmer in summer, and a little cooler in winter, but every day is a beach day for somebody.

There are no **strangers** in Paradise. Perhaps the most beautiful part of Hawaii is the genuine warmth of people. *We call it the spirit of Aloha. It has allowed a melting pot of cultures from all over the world to find common ground, and a new home, in this most* **gentle** *of places.*

　　对于大多数人来说，那些星星点点的关于夏威夷的印象，足以让我们沉浸在她的魅力之中了。金色的海滩、金色的人们。阳光、沙滩、大海、浪花……在蓝天和棕榈树之间，我们流连忘返。

　　夏威夷群岛是世界上最美丽的地方之一。这里气候怡人，气温常年在华氏 60 ～ 90 度之间。冬暖夏凉，对于某些人来说每天都是晒太阳的好日子。

　　在这个人间天堂，人们不会有陌生感。也许夏威夷人与生俱来的热情才是这里的真正魅力之所在。我们称之为爱的精神。作为世界上最文明地方之一的夏威夷，同时也是个多元文化的大熔炉。

❧单词注释❧

glimmer ['glimə] *v.* 发出微光；闪烁不定

temperature ['tempritʃə(r)] *n.* 温度，气温

stranger ['streindʒə] *n.* 陌生人；外地人

gentle ['dʒentl] *adj.* 温和的；和善的，仁慈的

❧实用句型 & 词组❧

The young woman was determined to hook a husband. （欺骗）

The temperature ranges between 30 and 40 degrees centigrade. （变动，变化）

One color melted into another. （逐渐变成）

❧翻译行不行❧

对于大多数人来说，那些星星点点的关于夏威夷的印象，足以让我们沉浸在她的魅力之中了。

_____

夏威夷群岛是世界上最美丽的地方之一。

_____

我们称之为爱的精神。作为世界上最文明地方之一的夏威夷，同时也是个多元文化的大熔炉。

_____

Spotlight on Copenhagen

美不胜收的哥本哈根

Are you too old for **fairy** tales? If you think so, Copenhagen is sure to change your mind.

See the city first from the water. *In the harbor sits Denmark's best-known landmark: the Little Mermaid.* Remember her? She left the world of the Sea People in search of a human soul in one of Hans Christian Andersen's beloved fantasies. From the harbor you can get a feel for the attractive "city of green spires." At twilight or in cloudy weather, the copper-covered spires of old castles and churches lend the city a dream-like **atmosphere**. You'll think you've stepped into a watercolor painting.

Copenhagen is a city on a human scale. You don't have to hurry to walk the city's center in less than an hour. Exploring it will take much longer. But that's easy. Copenhagen was the first city to declare a street for pedestrians only. *The city has less traffic noise and pollution than any other European capital.*

Stroll away from the harbor along the riverbanks, you'll see the modest Amalienborg Palace first. Completed in the mid—18th century, it still houses the royal family. The Danish Royal Guard is on duty. At noon, you ll watch the changing of the guard. The guards are not just for show, however. Danes will always remember their heroism on April 9, 1940. When the Nazis invaded Denmark, the guards aimed their guns and fired. Soldiers fell on both sides. The guards would all have been killed if the king hadn't ordered them to **surrender**.

Churches and castles are almost all that remain of the original city. Copenhagen became the capital of Denmark in 1445. During the late 16th century, trade grew, and so did the city. But fires in 1728 and 1795 destroyed the old wooden structures. Much of what we see today dates from the 19th and early 20th centuries.

See one of the spires up close—really close—at the 17th-century Church of Our Savior. Brave souls may climb the 150 stairs winding outside the spire to its top. If you're afraid of heights, or if it's a windy day, you can forget the climb. But then you'll miss the magnificent view.

Once the earth is under your feet again (you'll enjoy the feeling), cross the nearest **bridge** to Castle Island. The curious yet majestic—looking spire ahead tops the oldest stock exchange in Europe, built in 1619. Its spire is formed from the entwined tails of three dragons. They represent Denmark, Sweden and Norway.

Keep going, to the Christiansborg Palace. The town of Copenhagen began here. Stop and visit the medieval castle. Parliament and the Royal Reception Chambers are open, too. Then continue to Nyhavn, a narrow waterway dug by soldiers in 1673. You'll understand why Hans Christian Andersen made this charming waterway his home. A specially—built mirror outside his apartment window allowed him to peek unseen at the world outside.

Nyhavn is peaceful, an ideal place for lingering and people-watching. You'll usually see them dressed **casually**, though they are among Europe's rich people.

To see them having fun, and to have some fun yourself, cross Andersens Boulevard and enter Tivoli Gardens. You won't be alone. More than five million people a year come here. They come to dance, dine, take in outdoor and indoor concerts, see ballets and laugh at the comedy. One tip: Bring a lot of money. About 20 restaurants are among the city's most expensive. *Even without money, you can still enjoy the proud old trees, the colored night lights and the beautiful gardens. You might feel as if you are in a fairy tale.*

你是不是年龄大了，都不想看童话了？如果你是这么认为的话，哥本哈根一定能够改变你的想法。

要看这座城市，得先从水看起。丹麦最有名的标志性建筑——小美人鱼就坐落在港口处。记得她吗？在安徒生的一个童话里，她离开了海底世界，想变成一个真正的人。安徒生的许多童话故事都很受欢迎哩。从这个港口你可以领略到这座迷人的"绿色塔尖之城"的魅力。黎明时分或天气阴霾时，旧堡垒和教堂的镀铜塔尖会给这个城市营造梦一般的气氛。你会以为自己步入了一幅水彩画。

哥本哈根是一个很人性化的城市。你不需要在一小时内匆匆地将市中心走完。考察这个城市要花些时间。但那也是件很轻松的事。哥本哈根是第一个划出步行街的城市。跟欧洲其他国家的首都相比，这个城市的交通噪音和污染少了许多。

自港口沿着河岸漫步，最先映入眼帘的是风格朴实的阿玛利安堡皇宫。阿玛利安堡皇宫建造于 18 世纪中期，皇室家族至今仍居住于此。皇家卫队也还在这里执行任务。中午可以观赏到卫兵换岗的仪式。这些卫兵绝不仅是装装样子而已。丹麦人永远记得他们在 1940 年 4 月 9 日的英勇事迹。当时纳粹分子入侵丹麦，这里的卫兵与之开火交战。双方都有伤亡。如果不是国王下令让他们投降的话，这些卫兵可能全都为国捐躯了。

大概只有教堂与古堡是古城遗留下来的。哥本哈根于 1445 年成为丹麦的首都。16 世纪末，贸易的发展带动了城市的发展。但是，城中的旧式木制建筑在 1728 年和 1795 年的两场大火中毁于一旦。今天我们所看到的大部分建筑都是在 19 世纪和 20 世纪初建造的。

仔细看其中一个塔尖——真正靠近去看——这座建于 17 世纪的名为"我们的救世主"的教堂。勇敢的人可能会爬上那在尖塔外蜿蜒而上直通塔顶的 150 层阶梯。如果你恐高，或者当天的风很大，那就免了吧。不过，你会因此而错过那壮观的景色。

当你再次站在地面时（你会喜欢这种感觉的），你可以通过最近的桥到城堡岛。前方有个 1619 年建造的欧洲最古老的证券交易中心，上面的塔尖奇特而又宏伟。塔尖由三只龙尾缠绕而成，分别代表丹麦、瑞典和挪威。

继续往前，走到基斯汀堡。哥本哈根源自此处。停下来游览这个中世纪的古堡。议院和皇家接待室也同样开放，然后继续往尼哈芬走，它是 1673 年由士兵挖掘的一条狭窄水道。你会明白为什么汉斯·克里斯蒂安·安徒生会把这个迷人的水道当成自己的家。通过公寓窗外的一面特制的镜子，他能够看到外面的世界而又不被人发现。

尼哈芬是个宁静的地方，它也是个逗留和观看行人的理想之地。虽然他们是欧洲的有钱人，但是穿着都很随意。

要看丹麦人嬉乐，要想自己找点乐趣，你可以穿过安徒生大道，进入提弗利花园，在这儿你是不会寂寞的。每年有 500 多万人来此旅游。他们来这里跳舞、就餐、欣赏户外和室内音乐会，看芭蕾舞表演和喜剧。给你一个建议：多带些钱。这里有 20 多家本城最昂贵的餐厅。即使没有钱，你仍可以欣赏那些骄傲的老树、五光十色的彩灯，以及美丽的花园。你会觉得自己已置身于童话故事中了。

❦单词注释❦

fairy ['fɛəri] *n.* 小妖精；仙女

atmosphere ['ætməsfiə] *n.* 大气；空气

surrender [sə'rendə] *v.* 使投降，使自首

bridge [bridʒ] *n.* 桥，桥梁

casually ['kæʒjuəli] *adv.* 偶然地；无意地

❦实用句型 & 词组❦

I usually go on duty at 8 a.m.（值班；上班）

This is an original painting by Picasso.（原作的；原本的）

She was afraid that she might lose her job.（害怕的，怕的）

❦翻译行不行❦

丹麦最有名的标志性建筑——小美人鱼就坐落在港口处。

_____

跟欧洲其他国家的首都相比，这个城市的交通噪音和污染少了许多。

_____

即使没有钱，你仍可以欣赏那些骄傲的老树、五光十色的彩灯，以及美丽的花园。你会觉得自己置身于童话故事中了。

_____

The Allure and Charm of Paris

巴黎，浪漫之都

Ah, beautiful Paris. *For centuries this city has attracted the admiration of the world.* The allure and charm of Paris captivate all who visit there.

Where can you discover the charm of Paris for yourself? Is it in the legacy of this beautiful city ? Is it in the famous castles, palaces, statues and monuments, such as the Eiffel Tower? Can you find it in the world-class museums, such as the Louvre? Perhaps Paris'**allure** lies in the zest and style of the Parisians.

When you visit Paris, you don't have to spend all of your time visiting museums and monuments. They are certainly worthy of your time, but ignore them for a day. First take some time to look around and experience life in Paris. You'll find it charming.

Take a stroll along the Seine River. Browse through the art vendors, colorful paintings. Peek through delicate iron gates at the well-kept gardens. *Watch closely for the French attention to detail that has made France synonymous with good taste.*

You will see it in the design of a doorway or arch and in the Little fountains and quaint balconies. *No matter where you look*, *you will find everyday objects transformed into works of art.*

Spend some time in a quiet park relaxing on an old bench. Lie on your back on the green grass. When you need refreshment, try coffee and pastries at a sidewalk cafe. Strike up a conversation with a Parisian. This isn't always easy, though. With such a large international population living in Paris, true natives are hard to find these days.

As evening comes to Paris, **enchantment** rises with the mist over the riverfront. You may hear music from an outdoor concert nearby: classical, jazz, opera or chansons, those French folk songs. Parisians Love their music. The starry sky is their auditorium. You can also hear concerts in the chateaux and cathedrals. In Paris the Music never ends.

Don't miss the highlight of the Paris evening: eating out. Parisians are **proud** of their cuisine. And rightly so ;it's world famous. Gourmet dining is one of the indispensable joys of living. You need a special guidebook to help you choose one of the hundreds of excellent restaurants. The capital of France boasts every regional specialty, cheese and wine the country has to offer. If you don't know what to order, ask for the suggested menu. The chef likes to showcase his best dishes there. Remember, you haven't tasted the true flavor of France until you've **dined** at a French restaurant in Paris.

After your gourmet dinner, take a walking tour of the floodlit monuments. Cross the Pont Neuf, the oldest bridge in the city, to the Ile de la Cite. The most famous landmark of Paris looms up in front of you the Notre Dame Cathedral (Cathedral of Our Lady). Stand in the square in front of the cathedral. Here, you are standing in the center of France. All distances are **measured** from the front of Notre Dame. Every road in France leads to her front door. Notre Dame is the heart of Paris and the heart of France.

　　啊，美丽的巴黎！几个世纪以来，这个城市让整个世界对它心生羡慕。巴黎的诱惑与魅力吸引了所有到此游玩的人。

　　巴黎在哪些地方吸引你呢？是这座美丽城市的遗迹呢？还是那些有名的城堡、皇宫雕像和纪念碑，例如艾菲尔铁塔？亦或是像卢浮宫这样的世界一流博物馆呢？或许巴黎的诱惑力在于巴黎人的特殊品味和风格。

　　当你到巴黎游玩时，别把时间全都花在博物馆和纪念碑上面。它们绝对值得你看，但今天先忘掉它们吧。首先来四处看看，并体验一下巴黎的生活。你会发现它的迷人之处。

　　当你沿着塞纳河漫步时，你可以观赏艺术家们丰富多彩的绘画。透过那些精致的铁门，你可以看到里面精心呵护的花园。法国人很关注细节，这使得法国成为"好品味"的代名词。你可以从门廊、拱门、小喷泉和古怪有趣的走廊的设计上看到这一点。不管你往哪里看，你都能发现日常物品已经被他们变成了艺术品。

　　你可以花些时间，在一个安静的公园里的旧板凳上放松一下。你也可以躺在青草地上。想吃点心的时候，尝尝路边咖啡店的咖啡和点心。找一个巴黎人展开一段会话，但这也不太容易。在这个国际化的大都市里，想找到一个巴黎本地人并不是件易事。

到了傍晚时分，随着码头上的雾气升起，巴黎的诱惑力也随之而起。你也会听到附近室外音乐会所演奏的乐曲。古典、爵士、歌剧或是香颂、即法国的民歌。巴黎人热爱自己的音乐，繁星点缀的天空，就是他们演奏的大礼堂。你也可以在城堡或教堂里聆听音乐会。在巴黎，音乐是不会停止的。

别错过了巴黎夜晚的精彩节目：下馆子。巴黎人对其烹饪是非常自豪的。理当如此，因为它世界闻名。美食本来就是与生活享乐不可分割的。为了帮你在几百家绝佳的餐厅中作出选择，你需要一本特别的指南。法国的首都以各地的特色风味、乳酪和酒著称于世，如果你不知道该点什么，可以要菜单来看。大厨喜欢在此将他最拿手的菜作一番橱窗展示。请记住，在你尚未在巴黎的法国餐厅里吃过饭之前，都不算尝过真正的法国风味。

在你的美食晚餐之后，可以去看看被聚光灯照耀的纪念碑。穿过第九桥，这座巴黎最古老的桥，到达城市之岛。巴黎最有名的标志即隐约地呈现在你的面前：圣母院。站在教堂前面的广场，你即处于法国的正中心。所有的距离皆是以圣母院前门开始计算。法国的每一条路都通往它的前门。圣母院是巴黎的中心，也是法国的中心。

🌿单词注释🌿

allure [ə'ljuə] *v.* 引诱，诱惑

enchantment [in'tʃɑːntmənt] *n.* 魅力，迷人之处

proud [praud] *adj.* 骄傲的，有自尊心的

dine [dain] *v.* 进餐，用餐

measure ['meʒə] *v.* 测量；计量

🌿实用句型 & 词组🌿

A generator transforms mechanical energy into electricity.（使变换）

The miners are asking for another increase in pay.（要求）

A crowd gathered in front of the building.（在……的前面）

🌿翻译行不行🌿

几个世纪以来，这个城市吸引了整个世界的崇拜。

_____

法国人很关注细节，这使得法国成为"好品味"的代名词。

_____

不管你往哪里看，你都能发现日常物品已经被他们变成了艺术品。

_____

摩登时代
Modern times

Color Psychology，Do Different Colors Affect Your Mood? 每天懂一点色彩心理学

David Johnson

Like death and taxes，there is no escaping color. It is **ubiquitous**. Yet what does it all mean? Why are people more relaxed in green rooms? Why do weightlifters do their best in blue gyms?

Colors often have different meanings in various cultures. In the U.S., researchers have generally found the following to be accurate.

Black

Black is the color of authority and power. It is popular in fashion because it makes people appear thinner. It is also **stylish** and timeless. Black also implies submission. Priests wear black to signify submission to God. Some fashion experts say a woman wearing black implies submission to men. Black outfits can also be overpowering. or make the wearer seem aloof or evil. Villains. such as Dracula, often wear black.

White

Brides wear white to symbolize innocence and purity. *White is popular in decorating and in fashion because it is light, neutral, and goes with everything.* However, white shows dirt and is therefore more difficult to keep clean than other colors. Doctors and nurses wear white to imply sterility.

Red

The most emotionally intense color, red stimulates a faster **heartbeat** and breathing. It is also the color of love. Red clothing gets noticed and makes the wearer appear heavier. Since it is an extreme color, red clothing might not help people in negotiations or confrontations. Red cars are popular targets for thieves. In decorating, red is usually used as an accent. Decorators say that red furniture should be perfect since it will attract attention.

The most romantic color, pink, is more tranquilizing.

Blue

The color of the sky and the ocean, blue is one of the most popular colors. It causes the opposite reaction as red. Peaceful, tranquil blue causes the body to produce calming chemicals, so it is often used in bedrooms. Fashion consultants recommend wearing blue to job interviews because it symbolizes loyalty. People are more productive in blue rooms. Studies show weightlifters are able to handle heavier weights in blue gyms.

Green

Currently the most popular decorating color, green symbolizes nature. It is a calming, refreshing color. People waiting to appear on TV sit in "green rooms" to relax. Hospitals often use green because it relaxes patients. Brides in the Middle Ages wore green to symbolize fertility. Dark green is masculine, conservative. and implies wealth.

Yellow

Cheerful sunny yellow is an attention getter. While it is considered an optimistic color, people lose their tempers more often in yellow rooms, and babies will cry more. Yellow enhances concentration. hence its use for legal pads. It also speeds metabolism.

Purple

The color of royalty, purple connotes luxury, wealth, and sophistication. However, because it is rare in nature, purple can appear artificial.

Brown

Solid, reliable brown is the color of earth and is abundant in nature. Light brown implies genuineness while dark brown is similar to wood or leather. Brown can also be sad and wistful. Men are more apt to say brown is one of their favorite colors.

Colors of the Flag

In the U.S, flag, white stands for **purity** and innocence. Red represents valor and hardiness. while blue signifies justice, perseverance, and vigilance. The stars represent the heavens and all the good that people strive for, while the stripes emulate the sun's rays.

While blue is one of the most popular colors, it is one of the least appetizing. Blue food is rare in nature. Food researchers say that when humans searched for food, they learned to avoid toxic or spoiled objects, which were often blue, black, or purple. When food dyed blue is served to study subjects. they lose appetite.

Green, brown, and red are the most popular food colors. Red is often used in restaurant decorating schemes because it is an appetite stimulant.

颜色，如同死亡和税收一样，也是无处不在。那么，不同的颜色又代表了什么不同的含义呢？为什么人们在绿色的房间里会感到心情舒畅？为什么举重运动员在蓝色的体育馆内表现得非常出色呢？

在不同的文化背景中，颜色所表达的意义也有所不同。在美国，研究者对颜色的含义进行了精准的描述。

黑色

黑色是权威与权力的象征。它之所以是时装的流行色，是因为黑色的衣服使人看起来更苗条。黑色是永恒的时尚。黑色也意味着服从。神父身着黑色象征着对上帝的恭顺。一些服装设计师说，一个女人身着黑色意味着对男人的服从。黑色套装会使人感到难以抗拒，也会令人感到冷漠或邪恶。像德古拉，这个吸血鬼的化身，经常身着黑色。

白色

新娘身披白色婚纱，是天真和纯洁的象征。白色，因其明快、中性和随和而流行于世。但白色易脏，因此与其他颜色相比更难保持清洁。医护人员身着白色暗示着洁净无菌。

红色

红色是最具有激情的颜色，能加快人的心跳和呼吸。红色也是爱的色彩。红色服装引人注目，使穿着者显得厚重。由于其色彩过于艳丽，不适于在谈判或对抗性活动中穿着。红色轿车是窃贼的首选目标。在美化装潢方面，红色常是着重强调的色彩。装潢师说，因为红色会引起人们的注意，所以红色的家具会很理想。

最具浪漫色彩的是粉红色，它更能让人感到温馨。

蓝色

蓝色是天空和海洋的颜色，是最受人们喜爱的色彩之一。蓝色和红色相对应，宁静的蓝色会使人体产生令人镇定的化学物质。因此其适合用于卧室。时装顾问建议在面试时身着蓝色衣服，因为它代表着忠诚。人们在蓝色的房间内工作效率会更高。研究表明，举重运动员在蓝色场馆内的表现更佳。

绿色

目前，绿色是最时尚的装饰颜色，绿色代表着大自然。绿色使人安逸，令人振奋。人们在准备录节目的时候，坐在"绿色的房间"里，能放松心情。医院里通常是绿色基调，因为它会缓解病人的痛苦。中世纪的新娘身着绿色象征着她们的生育能力。墨绿色代表着阳刚、传统和财富。

黄色

欢快的金黄能吸引人们的注意力。人们把它看成是乐观向上的颜色。在黄色的房间里，人们更容易发脾气，婴儿也更容易哭闹。因为黄色能提高人们的注意力，所以它被用于警示牌。黄色还能加速人体的新陈代谢。

紫色

紫色代表着王室，意味着华贵、财富和权威。可是，在大自然中这种颜色很少见，所以紫色可能是人造的色彩。

棕色

在大自然中，坚固、结实的棕色是大地的色彩。它随处可见。树木和皮革的颜色接近于深褐色，而浅棕色才是正宗的棕色。棕色也能给人带来忧伤和渴望。男人更倾向于把棕色作为他们最喜欢的颜色之一。

旗帜的颜色

在美国国旗中，白色代表纯洁和天真。红色代表勇气和顽强，而蓝色象征正义、不屈不挠和机警。星星代表天堂和为美好未来而奋斗的人们，条纹代表太阳的光芒。

食物的随想

尽管蓝色是最受欢迎的颜色之一，但它同时也是最不能引起食欲的颜色之一。在自然界，蓝色食品是非常稀有的。食物研究人员说，当人们在寻找食物时，他们学会了避开有毒的或是腐烂的食物，而这些食物的颜色通常就是蓝色，黑色或紫色。每当看到食物呈蓝色时，他们就没了胃口。

绿色，棕色和红色是最流行的食物的颜色。餐馆在装修时，经常选用红色，因为红色能刺激人们的食欲。

正确选择宴会服装

越来越多的派对、宴会请柬特意标明"请穿着正式服装"。这时，为自己置备几套正装，就显得尤为必要了。而若是突然遇到必须着正装的场合，脑海中备着以下几招，更是有用，即挑选黑色永不落伍；配件作用不可小觑；小背心最是管用；懒人赴会中装讨巧；拒绝所有卡通。

🌿单词注释🌿

ubiquitous [juː'bikwitəs] *adj.* 到处存在的，普遍存在的

stylish ['stailiʃ] *adj.* 时髦的，流行的

heartbeat ['hɑːtbiːt] *n.* 心跳

purity ['pjuəriti] *n.* 纯净，清洁

🌿实用句型 & 词组🌿

I am used to walking to school. (习惯于)

She should be here any minute. (可能，该)

The country is abundant in natural resources. (丰富的；富裕的)

🌿翻译行不行🌿

颜色，如同死亡和税收一样，也是无处不在。

_____

白色，因其明快、中性和随和而流行于世。

_____

蓝色是天空和海洋的颜色，是最受人们喜爱的色彩之一。

_____

The Black Stretch

带上车子去散步

The impression of being in a pleasant cocoon, far from real life, is heightened by the **decisive** use of the glass partition between you and the driver. If your previous experience of partitions has been the greasy Plexiglas in taxis, which forces you to bellow your instructions at the driver and makes payment of the fare a process of crushed fingers and muttered oaths, the limo partition will come as a revelation to you. *One touch of the button in your armrest and the conversation-proof glass hisses up and stops communication dead.* (All professional drivers, for some reason, love to chat. Don't tolerate it. You're not paying all that money to listen to a lecture on Bush's fiscal policies.)

So there you are, a million miles from those yahoos on the street, immune from the weather, protected from small talk from the cockpit, going wherever you want to go in your own controlled environment. A perfect setting for a romantic **assignation**.

Women love limos. The minute they settle back in the seat they feel pampered and relaxed. They mentally dab a little scent behind each knee. They take a little more to drink than usual. They tend to lean toward you and whisper. They bloom. A date in a stretch is more intimate, more impressive, and far less prone to distraction than a movie and a candle–lit dinner. It is an extremely focused occasion.

A word of warning here. Whether on pleasure or business, it is important to observe chauffeur protocol, and this means curbing your natural warmth. We're not suggesting rudeness ; distant politeness will do very well. In other words, don't try to shake hands with your chauffeur or ask him how he's doing. Don't encourage him to address you by your first name. And don't ever open the door yourself, even if you have to wait a minute or two while he walks down the length of the car to let you out. These boys are pros, and they respect a pro passenger.

After one or two outings, you will probably start to become more specific in your requirements. You won't want any old limo. You'll want a limo in which the details are exactly right. A compact–disc player instead of a tape deck. Leather upholstery rather than cloth. Single–malt scotch, a freshly ironed copy of The Wall Street Journal, a Fax machine, a silver vase of freesias—once you get into the refinements, you'll never want to get out. But these come later.

While, as we have stated, only a black limo will do, we draw the line at black–tinted windows, for two reasons. First, they encourage autograph hunters, who will sidle up when the car is stopped at a light and peer at you and possibly mistake you for Mick Jagger or, worse, Ivan F. Boesky. And second, they make it **virtually** impossible for your friends—or, better still, your enemies—to catch a glimpse of you as you place phone calls and come to grips with the crystal decanters. Clear-glass windows are our recommendation, but it's a matter of personal choice.

In the stretch business, as in most other businesses, there exists a reduced-price trial offer. It works like this: let's say that you find yourself in Manhattan at the corner of Fifty-fifth and Third one evening around 6:30. All the cabs are taken, but if you make yourself sufficiently **obvious** as a man in need of transport, it won't be long before a prowling limo slows down. Hail it. Providing the driver likes the look of you, he'll stop, because he's just dropped his passenger and has a couple of hours to kill before picking him up again. Imbued with the spirit of enterprise, the driver will want to use this time profitably. As long as your destination won't make him late for his pickup, nobody will be the wiser and he'll be a little richer. The exact price should be agreed on before you get in, but you can be sure that it will be less than a formal arrangement with the limo company.

One trip is all it will take to make you start juggling your disposable income to pay for further expeditions, until the day comes when you will be ready to enjoy the ultimate refinement: taking your stretch for a walk.

A stroll of two or three blocks on a fine spring evening, the great black beast crawling obediently to heel, the bar stocked and waiting, the chauffeur alert to your beckoning finger, a ripple of envy through less fortunate **pedestrian**s marking your progress—now, there's a way to work up an appetite for dinner.

在你和司机之间断然加装上一道玻璃隔断，一定会更加让你觉得，自己像是蜗居在惬意的蚕茧里，远远隔离在真实世界之外。你以前领教过的士车厢里的隔断吧，是那种油腻腻的树脂玻璃。假如你有事要吩咐司机，都得扯开喉咙大吼；付钱时，手指头也常会卡在洞口，令你忍不住嘟嘟嚷嚷地诅咒一番。但豪华轿车内的隔断就不一样了，于你而言简直是天赐福音。只要轻触一下座椅扶手上的按键，隔音玻璃窗便嘶嘶作响，迅速升起，谈话也就此隔开。（职业司机不知为什么，个个都爱跟人聊天。是可忍，孰不可忍。你付这么些钱，并不是为了听司机就布什的财政政策神侃一通。）

所以，你坐在大轿车里，离大街上那些凡夫俗子相距十万八千里，既不受气候影响，也免遭来自驾驶座的闲话絮叨。爱去哪儿，就去哪儿，而且尽在你的掌控之中。这儿可真是赴浪漫之约的绝佳场所啊。

女士都爱豪华大轿车。她们一靠在座位上，那种备受娇宠、身心松弛的感觉便油然而生。在心理上，就如同在双膝下擦了些许香水，而且酒喝得也比平常多了一点。这时，她们喜欢依偎着你柔声耳语，好像绽放的花朵一般。在大轿车里约会，和看电影、吃烛光晚餐比起来，更容易亲近，更能打动芳心，也可免受外来干扰。在这样的情境里，她们绝不会心有旁骛。

在此必须提醒一句，无论你是去寻欢作乐，还是洽谈公务，请务必遵守乘车须知。这么说的意思是希望你克制一下你天性中的温情主义。我们不是要你粗鲁无礼，而是要你保持有距离的礼貌。换言之，不要跟你的司机握手或寒暄，问他近来可好；不可以让他直接叫你的名字；也绝不要自己动手开门。宁可等上一两分钟，你也要让他走过一辆车长的距离来为你开门。这些人都是行家，他们敬重的，也必定是那些内行的乘客。

有过一两次出游之后，你可能就会开始提出特别的要求了。你不会要一辆旧车。你要的车，其中的设施、细节必须完全符合你的要求才行。比如说，音响一定是 CD 播放机，不可以是卡式录音机；车内一定要用真皮装饰，不可以是布艺的；还须有单一麦芽型的苏格兰威士忌，一份刚熨烫过的《华尔街日报》，一架传真机，以及插在银瓶内的小苍兰——一旦陷入这种精致的享受当中，你恐怕永远不会弃之而去了。但这些不妨留待后话再叙。

尽管一开始就提到，这豪华大轿车非黑色莫取，但我们对黑色的玻璃车窗可要仔细掂量一下。原因有二：第一，黑玻璃窗可能引来签名搜集狂。车子一停在红灯前，他们便会悄悄贴近，由车外盯着你看，搞不好会误认你是摇滚明星麦克·杰格。要不更糟，把你当成了华尔街套汇高手伊凡·波伊斯基。第二，这黑玻璃让你的朋友——或者最好是你的敌人，几乎不可能看见你人坐在车内，正放下电话，要伸手去抓水晶酒瓶。所以我们建议用透明的玻璃窗，不过这纯属个人自由。

和其他大部分行业一样，在豪华大轿车租赁这一行里，都有特惠试用的优待。做法是这样的：假设你在傍晚六点半左右，发现自己身陷曼哈顿 55 街和第三大道的交叉口，而所有的出租车都已有人乘坐。这时，如果你摆出一副急需打车走人的模样，而且相当显眼，那么过不了多久，就会有一辆匍匐潜行的大轿车开始放慢速度接近你。招手叫它。那司机若看你顺眼，就会停下车来。因为他刚刚送完客人，再去接人之前还有几个小时要打发呢。这些司机骨子里浸透了商人意识，多半会利用这段档期挣钱的。只要你去的地方不耽误他去接人，没有人会傻到有钱不赚一把的。你在上车前一定要先谈妥确切的价钱。但你尽可以放心，这价钱肯定比你向租车公司租车要低得多。

只要坐上一次，你就会一发不可收地在你的可支配收入里凑出钱来再坐上几次。这样，终有一天，你会品味到那极至的享受：带上车子去散步。

这是一个美好的春夜。你乘车悠闲地穿过两三个街区。那又黑又大的四轮兽顺从地匍匐在你的脚跟下。车内吧台、饮品、用具一一备齐，只等着你就坐。你只需稍稍动一下手指头，司机便会随时听候你的吩咐。所经之处，一阵阵艳羡的涟漪在那些命运不济的行人之中荡漾——现在，该是调动你的胃口，好好享用晚餐的时候了！

单词注释

decisive [di'saisiv] *adj.* 决定性的，决定的
assignation [,æsig'neiʃən] *n.* 分配，分派
virtually ['vɜ:tjuəli] *adv.* 实际上，事实上，差不多
obvious ['ɔbviəs] *adj.* 明显的；显著的
pedestrian [pe'destriən] *adj.* 徒步的，步行的

实用句型 & 词组

Manchester is farther from London than Oxford is. (遥远的；久远的)
You should sleep more than you do. (更多；更大程度地)
The machine slowed down and stopped. (变慢)

翻译行不行

只要轻触一下座椅扶手上的按键，隔音玻璃窗就嘶嘶作响，迅速升起，谈话也就此隔开。

女人都爱豪华大轿车。她们一靠在座位上，那种备受娇宠、身心松弛的感觉便油然而生。

只要坐上一次，你就会一发不可收地在你的可支配收入里凑出钱来再坐上几次。这样，终有一天，你会品味到那极至的享受：带上车子去散步。

岁月流逝，感怀永存：经典电影台词

It takes a strong man to save himself, and a great man to save another.

Hope is a good thing, maybe the best of things, and no good thing ever dies.

Life was like a box of chocolate, you never know what you're gonna get.

It was like just before the sun goes to bed down on the bayou.There was a million sparkles on the river.

If there is anything you need I will not be far away.

It's my time. It's just my time. Oh, now, don't you be afraid sweetheart. Death is just a part of life, something we're all destined to do. I didn't know it. But I was **destined** to be your momma. I did the best I could.

Everything you see exists together in a delicate balance.

I'm only brave when I have to be. Being brave doesn't mean you go looking for trouble.

When the world turns its back on you, you turn your back on the world.

This is my kingdom. If I don't fight for it, who will?

Land is the only thing in the world worth working for, worth fighting for, worth dying for. Because it's the only thing that lasts.

In spite of you and me and the whole **silly** world going to pieces around us, I love you.

Now I find myself in a world which for me is worse than death. A world in which there is no place for me.

You're throwing away happiness with both hands. And **reaching** out for something that will never make you happy.

God shall wipe away all the tears from their eyes, and there shall be no more death. Neither shall there be sorrow or dying, neither shall there be any more pain, for the former world has passed away.

Work hard! Work will save you. Work is the only thing that will see you through this.

You make millions of decisions that mean nothing and then one day your order takes out and it changes your life.

Destiny takes a hand.

People who truly loved once are far more likely to love again.

When you're **attracted** to someone it just means that your subconscious is attracted to their subconscious, subconsciously. So what we think of as fate, is just two neuroses knowing they're a perfect match.

I don't want to be someone that you're settling for. I don't want to be someone that anyone settles for.

坚强的人拯救自己，伟大的人救赎他人。

希望是美好的，也许是人间至善，而美好的事物永不消逝。

人生就像一盒巧克力，你永远不知道会尝到哪种滋味。

就像太阳在落山前映射在河口上，有无数的亮点在闪闪发光。

用情至专！

别害怕，死亡是生命的一部分，是我们注定要去做的一件事。我不知道怎么回事，但我注定是你的妈妈，并且我尽我的全力去做好。

世界上所有的生命都在微妙的平衡中生存。

我只是在必要的时候才会勇敢，勇敢并不代表你要到处闯祸。

如果这个世界对你不理不睬，你也可以这样对待它。

这是我的国土，我不为她战斗，谁来为她战斗呢？

土地是世界上唯一值得你去为之工作，为之战斗，为之牺牲的东西，因为它是唯一永恒的东西。

哪怕是世界末日我都会爱着你。

现在我发现自己活在一个比死还要痛苦的世界，一个没有我容身之处的世界。

你把自己的幸福拱手相让，去追求一些根本不会让你幸福的东西。

上帝擦去他们所有的眼泪，死亡不再有。也不再有悲伤和生死离别，不再有痛苦，因往事已矣。

努力工作吧！工作能拯救你。埋头苦干可令你忘记痛楚。

你每天都在做很多看起来毫无意义的决定，但某天你的某个决定就能改变你的一生。

命中注定。

真爱过的人很难再恋爱。

当你被某个人吸引时，那只是意味着你俩在潜意识里相互吸引。因此，所谓命运，就只不过是两个疯子认为他们自己是天造一对，地设一双。

我不想要你将就，我也不想成为将就的对象。

➤单词注释➤

destine ['destin] *v.* 命定，注定

silly ['sili] *adj.* 愚蠢的；糊涂的

reach [ri:tʃ] *v.* 抵达，到达；达到

attract [ə'trækt] *v.* 吸；吸引

➤实用句型 & 词组➤

The computer will save us a lot of time. （省去；避免）

It's too early for bed. （睡觉；就寝时间）

That novel is not worth reading. （值得）

➤翻译行不行➤

希望是美好的，也许是人间至善，而美好的事物永不消逝．

_____

这是我的国土，我不为她而战斗，谁来为她战斗呢？

_____

真爱过的人很难再恋爱。

_____

Views on Various Wedding Customs

全世界奇特的婚礼习俗

Armenia: *Two white doves may be released to signify love and happiness.* The bride may dress in red silk and may wear cardboard wings with feathers on her head. Small coins may be thrown at her.

Caribbean: A rich black cake baked with dried fruits and rum is especially popular on the islands of Barbados, Grenada and St. Lucia. It is considered a "pound" cake — with the recipe calling for a pound each of flour, dark brown sugar, butter, glace cherries, raisins, prunes, currants, plus a dozen eggs and flavorings. The dried fruits are soaked in rum and kept in a crock anywhere from two weeks to six months.

Croatia: Married female relatives remove the bride's veil and replace it with a kerchief and apron, symbols of her new married status. She is then **serenaded** by all the married women.

Following the wedding ceremony, those assembled walk three times around the well (symbolizing the Holy Trinity) and throw apples into it (symbolizing fertility).

The Czech Republic: Friends would sneak into the bride's yard to plant a tree, then decorate it with ribbons and painted eggshells. Legend said she would live as long as the tree. Brides in the countryside carry on the very old custom of wearing a wreath of rosemary, which symbolizes remembrance. The wreath is woven for each bride on her wedding eve by her friends as a wish for **wisdom**, love, and loyalty.

Egypt: Families, rather than grooms, propose to the bride. In Egypt, many marriages are arranged. The zaffa, or wedding march, is a musical **procession** of drums, bagpipes, horns, belly dancers, and men carrying flaming swords；it announces that the marriage is about to begin.

England: Traditionally, the village bride and her wedding party always walk together to the church. *Leading the procession: a small girl strewing, blossoms along the road, so the bride's path through life will always be happy and laden with flowers.*

Finland: Brides wear golden crowns. After the wedding, unmarried women dance in a circle around the blindfolded bride, waiting for her to place her crown on someone's head. It is thought that whoever she crowns will be the next to wed. The bride and groom have seats of honor at the reception. The bride holds a sieve covered with a silk shawl. when the guests slip money into the sieve, their names and the amounts given are announced to those assembled by a groomsman.

Greece: The koumbaros, traditionally the groom's godfather, is an honored guest who participates in the wedding ceremony.

Today, the koumbaros is very often the best man, who assists in the crowning of the couple (with white or gold crown, or with crowns made of **everlasting** flowers, or of twigs of love and vine wrapped in silver and gold paper), and in the circling of the altar three times. Other attendants may read Scripture, hold candles, pack the crowns in a special box after the ceremony. *To be sure of a "sweet life", a Greek bride may carry a lump of sugar in her glove on wedding day.*

亚美尼亚：人们放飞两只白鸽，以示爱情和幸福。新娘穿着红色丝质服装，头戴饰有羽毛的纸翼。人们还可向新娘投掷硬币。

加勒比地区：在巴巴多斯，格林纳达和圣卢西亚，用干果和朗姆酒制作的味道浓郁的蛋糕十分常见。人们把这种蛋糕称为"一磅"蛋糕，因为制作这种蛋糕需要面粉、红糖、黄油、糖霜樱桃、葡萄干、李子、红醋栗各一磅，加上一打鸡蛋和调味品。制作蛋糕的干果要在朗姆酒中浸泡并在瓦罐中保存两个星期至6个月。

克罗地亚：由已婚的女性亲戚摘下新娘的面纱，换成一块头巾和一条围裙，意味着新娘的已婚身份。然后由所有的已婚妇女为新娘唱小夜曲。婚礼仪式结束之后，所有来宾围绕着井走三圈（象征着圣父、圣子、圣灵三位一体），并向井中扔苹果（象征着生育）。

捷克共和国：朋友们溜进新娘的院子去种一棵树，然后再用彩带和彩绘的蛋壳将树加以装饰。传说新娘将与这棵树活得一样长。乡村的新娘还保留着佩带迷迭香花环的传统习俗，以表怀念之情。花环是在婚礼前夕由新娘的朋友编织而成，它象征着智慧、爱情和忠诚。

埃及：在埃及，由新郎的家人，而不是新郎本人，向新娘求婚。许多婚姻还是父母之命，媒妁之言。Zaffa，也就是婚礼，其实是一个有音乐伴奏的列队游行，有鼓、风笛、号角及肚皮舞，男人们手持火红的剑。这个仪式宣告婚姻即将开始。

英格兰：按照传统，乡村的新娘和参加婚礼的人们总是一起走向教堂。一个小姑娘走在队列的最前面，她一路抛撒鲜花，预示着新娘的一生幸福快乐，鲜花永伴。

芬兰：新娘头戴金色的花冠。婚礼后，未婚女子围着被蒙住眼睛的新娘跳舞，等着新娘将花冠戴到某个人的头上。被新娘戴上花冠的人被认为是下一个要结婚的人。新娘和新郎坐在婚宴的贵宾席上，新娘手持一个筛子，筛子上盖有一块丝绸披巾。当来宾们将钱塞进筛子时，一个伴郎会向在场的来宾宣布放钱的来宾姓名以及礼金的数额。

希腊：按照传统是由新郎的教父来担任婚礼的嘉宾。现在，嘉宾通常由伴郎担任，其职责是协助新郎新娘戴上花冠（花冠有白色和金色的，花冠由四季开放的鲜花，或由用金色或银色的纸包起来的象征爱情的树枝和藤编织而成）。戴上花冠后，新人们围着圣坛绕三圈。其他出席婚礼的宾客则手持蜡烛，朗读《圣经》，并在婚礼后将花冠放置在一个特殊的盒子里。为了婚后生活能甜蜜，希腊新娘在结婚那一天，可在手套里塞一块糖。

🌱单词注释🌱

signify ['signifai] *v.* 表示；表明

serenade [ˌseri'neid] *n.* 小夜曲；情歌

wisdom ['wizdəm] *n.* 智慧，才智，明智

procession [prə'seʃən] *n.* 一（长）列，一（长）排

everlasting [ˌevə'lɑːstiŋ] *adj.* 永远的，永久的；不朽的

🌱实用句型 & 词组🌱

I didn't notice Tom sneaking up behind me.（偷偷地走，溜）

The great hall was decorated with flowers.（装饰，修饰）

He rose to fetch a chair from the next room.（紧邻的，贴近的）

🌱翻译行不行🌱

人们放飞两只白鸽，以示爱情和幸福。

_____

一个小姑娘走在队列的最前面，她一路抛撒鲜花，预示着新娘的一生幸
福快乐，鲜花永伴。

_____

为了婚后生活能甜蜜，希腊新娘在结婚那一天，可在手套里塞一块糖。

_____

Britain's Got Talent—Susan Beyle

我曾梦想：英国超女成功记

*The Internet has not seen anything quite like Susan Boyle, whose online **popularity** is headed straight into the history books.*

The video of Boyle's performance on the reality show Britain's Got Talent has set the record for the number of views in a week—and it shows no sign of slowing down.

According to Visible Measures, which tracks videos from Youtube.com, Myspace.com and other video-sharing sites, all Boyle-oriented videos have generated a total of 85.2 million views.

Nearly 20 million of those views came overnight.

But it's not just in online video where Boyle, the unassuming woman from a tiny Scottish town, has **dominated**.

Over the weekend, her Facebook fan page was flooded with comments.

The page listed 150,000 members at 1 pm on April 10. By the night of April 12, there were more than a million.

Indeed, the sleepless Internet is her round–the–clock stage, and the 47–year–old who has said she's never heard of Youtube is the Web's hottest entertainer.

*To media observers, the speed and **scope** of Boyle's online ubiquity is a testament to the fact that the marriage between old media and new media is broadening the reach of all media – from one channel to another, from person to person.*

Her performance first aired on British TV then made its way to Youtube and Facebook.

"What we're really seeing with Susan Boyle is the power of 'spreadability'," according to Henry Jenkins, co–director of MIT's **comparative** media studies program.

"Consumers in their own online communities are making conscious choices to spread Susan Boyle around online," Jenkins said.

At any given moment, on any particular site, someone is passing along Boyle online.

Tanya Gold, the Guardian, Why are we so shocked when "ugly" women can do things, other than sitting at home weeping and wishing they were somebody else?

Susan will probably win Britain's Got Talent. ... But Susan Boyle will be the freakish exception that makes the rule.

By raising this Susan up, we will forgive ourselves for **grinding** every other Susan into the dust.

Mary Elizabeth Williams, Salon.com : When Boyle sings, our identification transfers instantly to her. She's us.

A regular, imperfect, unairbrushed person, an intimate friend of rejection and loneliness and mockery and disappointment. A person who, in spite of everything, clings resolutely to the conviction that there is something inside her that's very special.

在互联网上，像苏珊·鲍以尔这样一炮走红而被载入史册的人物可以说是史无前例了。

在短短一周内，浏览鲍以尔在《英国达人》中表演的视频人数已经创下了记录。而且，该数字丝毫没有回落的态势。

据专门追踪 Youtube、Myspace 等视频分享网站点击次数的 Visible Measures 报道，所有和鲍以尔相关的视频已经拥有高达 8,520 万的观众。

而其中，约 2,000 万观众是在一夜之间产生的。

然而，这位来自苏格兰小镇的随和大妈鲍以尔所主导的领域远不止在线视频。

仅一个周末的时间，她的 Facebook 粉丝页就几乎被评论所淹没。

4 月 10 日下午 1 点，页面显示有 15 万名粉丝，而到了 12 日晚间，该数字已超过 100 万。

事实上，互联网已经成了她全天候的舞台。而这位曾表示连 Youtube 都没听说过的 47 岁大妈也成了该网站最热的"艺人"。

对于媒体观察者们来说，鲍以尔串红互联网的速度之快，范围之广无不印证了一个事实：新旧媒体的结合能让更多人认识到所有媒体，从一个渠道到另一个渠道，从一个人到另外一个人。

她的表演起初在英国电视台播出，之后便登上了 Youtube 和 Facebook 的网站。

麻省理工学院比较媒介研究项目教授亨利·詹金斯表示："我们从苏珊·鲍以尔身上看到了'压倒一切'的能量。"

詹金斯还说："互联网用户们很自觉地在自己的网络社区中传播苏珊·鲍以尔。"

无论何时何地，总有人在网上传播着鲍以尔的消息。

《卫报》的网友 Tanya Gold 说：当我们看到"丑女"不再坐在家里哭泣，而是希望自己变成名人时，我们为何如此震惊？

苏珊很可能赢得《英国达人》的冠军，但是她将是开辟这个模式的一个罕见的例外。

另外，捧起苏珊，我们也能够原谅自己曾经取笑打击那些像苏珊这样的人。

网络杂志《沙龙》的 Mary Elizabeth Williams 说：鲍以尔唱歌的时候，我们在她身上找到了自己。

尽管她很普通，不完美，孤独失望并常遭别人奚落，但她总是坚信自己身上有特别之处。

单词注释

popularity [ˌpɔpjuˈlæriti] *n.* 普及，流行；大众化

dominate [ˈdɔmineit] *v.* 支配，统治，控制

scope [skəup] *n.* 范围，领域

comparative [kəmˈpærətiv] *adj.* 比较的；用比较方法的

grinding [ˈgraindiŋ] *adj.* 令人难以忍受的；恼人的

rejection [riˈdʒekʃən] *n.* 拒绝；退回；剔除

实用句型 & 词组

Their expenses reached a total of 1，000 pounds.（总数；合计）

The landlord raised my rent.（提高；提升）

We forgave him his rudeness.（原谅，宽恕）

翻译行不行

在互联网上，像苏珊·鲍以尔这样一炮走红计入史册的人物可以说是史无前例了。

_____

对于媒体观察者们来说，鲍以尔串红互联网的速度之快，范围之广无不印证了一个事实：新旧媒体的结合能让更多人认识到所有媒体，从一个渠道到另一个渠道，从一个人到另外一个人。

_____

尽管她很普通，不完美，时常与孤独，别人的奚落和失望为伴，但她总是坚信自己身上有特别之处。

_____

Just One Last Dance

最后一支舞

Just one last dance. Oh baby, just one last dance

We meet in the night in the Spanish cafe

I look in your eyes just don't know what to say

It feels like I'm drowning in salty water

A few hours left till the sun's gonna rise

Tomorrow will come and it's time to **realize**: Our love has finished forever

How I wish to come with you! How I wish we make it through!

Just one last dance before we say goodbye.

When we sway and turn around around around. It's like the first time

Just one more chance. Hold me **tight** and keep me warm

Cause the night is getting cold and I don't know where I belong

Just one last dance

The wine and the lights and the Spanish guitar

I'll never forget how **romantic** they are

But I know, tomorrow I'll lose the one I love

There's no way to come with you. It's the only thing to do:

Just one last dance before we say goodbye

When we sway and turn around and round and round. It's like the first time

Just one more chance. Hold me tight and keep me warm

Cause the night is getting cold and I don't know where I belong

Just one last dance.

Just one last dance and just one more chance. Just one last dance.

再来最后一舞，亲爱的，再来最后的一舞

夜晚我们相遇在那个西班牙咖啡厅。

我望着你的双眸却欲说无言

我犹如在大海里挣扎。太阳就要升起

新的一天就要到来，可我们的爱却永远终止

我多么希望能随你而去！多么希望我们能共度此生！

在说再见之前，再来最后的一舞吧。

当我们转啊转啊转，就像第一次那样

再来一支舞吧，抱紧我，温暖我

因为夜已寒，而我却不知道自己将何处归。

再来最后一舞

美酒、华灯和这西班牙吉他的浪漫，此生难忘

我知道，明天我将失去我的所爱

我无法随你而去。现在唯一能做的：

就是离别前，再来最后的一舞。

就像第一次那样，我们一起转啊转啊转不停，

再来一支舞吧，抱紧我，温暖我

因为夜已寒，而我却不知道将何处归。再来最后一舞。

莎拉蔻娜（Sarah Connor）

德国歌手莎拉蔻娜，出道短短几年就获得德国乐坛最高荣耀"Echo 音乐奖"最佳流行摇滚女歌手，以及 VIVA Comet 奖最佳新进艺人等奖项。她的专辑《Sarah Connor》成功打进美国市场，并荣登潜力榜冠军、单曲 Bounce 获主流榜 Top11。

🌿单词注释🌿

drown [draun] *v.* 淹没，浸湿

realize ['riəlaiz] *v.* 领悟，了解，认识到

tight [tait] *adj.* 紧的，不松动的；牢固的

romantic [rə'mæntik] *adj.* 富于浪漫色彩的；虚构的；幻想的

🌿实用句型 & 词组🌿

I don't feel like a cup of tea.（想要）

The barren land has been turned into fertile fields.（使变化；改变）

Will this food keep in hot weather?（保持）

🌿翻译行不行🌿

我犹如在大海里挣扎。太阳就要升起。

_____

因为夜已寒，而我却不知道自己将何处归。

_____

再来一支舞吧，抱紧我，温暖我。

_____

Contemporary Jewellery Is More About Ideas Than the Flaunting of Wealth 当代首饰设计新理念

Through the centuries people have worn jewellery to depict status, wealth and identity. Now there is another reason. Contemporary jewellery, the kind that is fought over by passionate collectors, focuses as much on intellectual inquiry and the telling of stories as it does on the exploration of materials and techniques.

To the cognoscenti, contemporary jewellery is wearable sculpture, and the wearability of a piece and the way it moves on the body are of critical importance to the artists who create it. This work is a product of head, heart and hand, with the head element uppermost. Pieces can be made of anything: found objects, recycled junk, textiles, plastic—even paper. If they include precious metals and gemstones, these rarely appear in conventional forms. Collectors are mainly professionals. A significant proportion are architects and many of them are men.

*Humour and subversion are an **intrinsic** element of this kind* *of jewellery, which may explain why one European country, the Netherlands, has become a beacon for collectors.* As Marjan Unger, a Dutch art historian and jewellery curator, explains it, the Dutch "like to turn things upside down" . They possess a fierce merchant mentality, but do not like to display their wealth, preferring instead to show off their intellectual power.

The Netherlands boasts some fine jewellery schools, but, other than diamond-cutting, there is little historical tradition in jewellery making. Dutch designers have not had to fight entrenched conventions, and as a result they have been remarkably free to experiment.

"Collect" , an international fair for contemporary objects, which opens in London will show a number of artists who explore concepts of preciousness, value and beauty by subverting traditional materials and techniques. Some are German, Swiss and British, as well as Dutch. Otto Künzli famously made a rubber bracelet concealing a gold ball inside. Karl Fritsch ground gemstones into powder and reassembled them with glue. He is now experimenting with drilling holes in the gems and knotting them together in varying configurations. Gijs Bakker, co-founder of Droog, a design company, combines gemstones with costume pieces. Ulrich Reithofer combines gold and glass shards in a necklace.

Using unconventional materials is another way of questioning "value" . Dorothea Prühl uses wood to create huge neckpieces. Christoph Zellweger covers animal bones with flesh-coloured flock. Lisa Walker assembles three-dimensional collages using found plastic pieces and assembles them into wearable sculpture. Sebastian Buescher pins together eclectic **combinations** of materials he gathers outdoors.

Story-telling is another key element. The narratives vary from the personal to the collective, but individual memories are often used to tap into universal themes. The domestic is a favourite. Gesine Hackenberg drills out circles from discarded plates, configuring them into necklaces which she presents on the original, now disfigured, platters. Iris Eichenberg examines the psychological effect of transition to a new culture by assembling materials from different elements of an interior such as flooring, wall coverings and furniture into brooches and neck pieces. Francis Willemstijn even uses old car parts to allude to her childhood spent in her father's garage ; contrary to expectation, they make **exquisite** jewellery.

This is jewellery offering a very different expression of identity. The wearer of such pieces challenges preconceived notions. It can include a whiff of intellectual snobbery, *as the wearer can be seen as* "*buying a bit of the artist's brain*".

　　自古以来，人们佩戴首饰是为了显示地位、财富和身份。现在，佩戴首饰又有了别的涵义。热忱的收藏家对当代首饰的看法也不一样。当代首饰在探求材料和工艺的同时，也关注着文化内涵和叙事性。

　　对于鉴赏家来说，当代首饰是可以佩戴的艺术品。它对于创作首饰的艺术家来说，首饰的耐用性，和怎么佩戴都是至关重要的。它集创作者的思想、热情和工艺于一体，尤其以思想至上。任何东西都可以用来制作当代首饰：像锻造品、回收的废旧杂物、纺织品、塑料等等，甚至报纸也行。如果是含有贵金属和宝石的东西，它们则很少以传统造型亮相。收藏家主要是一些专业人士。设计师占了很大的比例，其中以男性为主。

幽默和颠覆性是此类首饰的本质内涵。这也许能解释为什么荷兰这个欧洲国家会成为收藏家的指路明灯。因为这正像荷兰艺术历史学家和首饰馆长 Marjan Unger 所说的，荷兰人"喜欢混淆黑白"。他们虽具敏锐的商业头脑，却不喜欢显露财富，更愿意表现才智。

虽然荷兰拥有一批引以为豪的高级首饰学校，但是在首饰制作（不包括钻石切割）上几乎没有什么历史传统。这样，荷兰的设计师就不必受制于传统，因此他们可以自由地去尝试。

"收藏展"将在伦敦举行。它是一个当代首饰作品的国际展览会，届时将有很多来自德国、瑞士、英国和荷兰的艺术家参展。通过颠覆传统的材料和技巧，他们将探究名贵、价值和美感这些概念。Otto Künzli 因制作了内部藏有金球的橡胶手镯而出名。Karl Fritsch 将宝石磨成粉末，然后用胶水粘结。他现在正尝试着在宝石上钻孔，然后扣接成不同的造型。Droog 设计公司的合伙人 Gijs Bakker，将宝石镶到了服装上。Ulrich Reithofer 用黄金和玻璃碎片制作了一条项链。

探究"价值"的另一个途径就是使用非传统材料。Dorothea Prühl 用木材做了许多硕大无比的项链挂件。Christoph Zellweger 用肉色毛绒包裹动物骨头。Lisa Walker 用塑料片组装成三维的拼贴画，并将此制成可以佩戴的雕塑品。Sebastian Buescher 将他在户外收集的各式各样的材料连接在一起。

叙事性是另一个重要的内涵。从个人到集体，叙事对象各不相同，但是个人的回忆经常用来创作大众性的主题。生活日用品是最受欢迎的主题。Gesine Hackenberg 从丢弃的盘子上钻出圆环，这原先被当做项链，而现在象征着破损的唱片。Iris Eichenberg 将不同的室内材料，例如地板、墙面装饰以及家具拼装成胸针和项链挂件，并通过这种新的尝试来检测对心理转变的影响。Francis Willemstijn 甚至利用汽车的废旧部件来暗示她在父亲车库里度过的童年。出乎意料的是，他们创作了精美的首饰。

这样一来，首饰就成了人们自我表达的一种方式。这些作品的佩戴者在冲击着人们的先入之见。佩戴者可被认为购买了艺术家的思想，因此它意味着才智的流露。

❧单词注释❧

depict [dɪˈpɪkt] *v.* 描画；雕出

intrinsic [ɪnˈtrɪnsɪk] *adj.* 本身的；本质的

combination [ˌkɔmbɪˈneɪʃən] *n.* 结合（体）；联合

exquisite [ˈekskwɪzɪt] *adj.* 精美的；精致的

❧实用句型 & 词组❧

That was a critical time in the nation's history.（关键性的，危急的）

They are turning waste land into paddy fields.（使变成）

He was seen to come out.（看见，看到）

❧翻译行不行❧

自古以来，人们佩戴首饰是为了显示地位、财富和身份。

———————————————————————————————

幽默和颠覆性是此类首饰的本质内涵。这也许能解释为什么荷兰这个欧洲国家会成为收藏家的指路明灯。

———————————————————————————————

这样一来，首饰就成了人们自我表达的一种方式。这些作品的佩戴者在冲击着人们的先入之见。佩戴者可被认为购买了艺术家的思想，因此它意味着才智的流露。

———————————————————————————————

The Influence of Cézanne

追踪大师：塞尚的影响力

Paul Cézanne, who died in 1906, cast a long shadow across 20th-century art. Pablo Picasso, who, with Georges Braque, invented **cubism**, called him "my one and only master". Henri Matisse, Picasso's rival for supreme **artist** of the modern period, described him as "a sort of god of painting".

Critics and scholars may disagree about pinpointing the first stirrings of modern art, but few deny Cézanne's pivotal role as midwife. His fracturing of form and flattening of space, especially evident in his landscapes and still lifes, laid the foundation for cubism, the revolutionary movement that planted **radical** ideas firmly in the minds of young painters in Europe and America.

Cézanne's influence was strongest during the generation after he died, but it has proved remarkably persistent. Only now, a century later, when electronic media such as photography and video have wrested control of the vanguard from painting, is Cézanne's shadow beginning to **fade**.

However, until mid-May he continues to display his authority at the Philadelphia Museum of Art, which has mounted an enchanting exhibition designed to validate the claims of Picasso, Matisse and 14 other legatees whose art has been shaped by Cézanne's example.

"Cézanne and Beyond" juxtaposes about 60 paintings and watercolours by the French master with roughly twice that many by the others: Europeans such as Piet Mondrian, Fernand Léger, Max Beckmann and Alberto Giacometti, and Americans—Marsden Hartley, Charles Demuth, Jasper Johns and Ellsworth Kelly.

The aim is to illuminate stylistic similarities and show how Cézanne expanded the way artists think. Confronted by such iconic subjects as Mont St Victoire near Cézanne's home in Aix-en-Provence and his magisterial still lifes of apples, they could no longer simply reproduce nature, they had to deconstruct it. The cubists provide the most **vivid** examples of this transformation but the most contemporary of the 16, especially Mr Kelly, Brice Marden and Canadian photographer Jeff Wall, have devised more subtle ways of incorporating Cézanne's principles into their work.

"Cézanne and Beyond" is a beautiful and powerful collection of modern and post-modern art by some of the most talented painters of the past 100 years. It is also the most impressive survey of Cézanne's painting in America since a 1996 retrospective, (also in Philadelphia as well as London and Paris). This time it is three exhibitions in one, courtesy of the last old Master.

保罗·塞尚死于1906年，他对整个二十世纪的艺术产生了深远的影响。开创了立体派的帕伯罗·毕加索，与乔治·布拉克都称他为"我心中独一无二的大师"。可与毕加索堪比为现代最高艺术家的亨利·马蒂斯，将他描述为"一种绘画艺术之神"。

评论家和学者们也许对确定现代艺术的开创者意见不一，但是几乎没有人否认塞尚作为助产士一样的关键作用。他使形状分裂，将空间压扁，在他的风景画与静物画中尤为明显，这为立体派奠定了基础。立体派是一种革命性的变化，它在欧美青年画家的心目中已深深扎根。

塞尚对他下一代人的影响是最强烈的，此外也被证实是极为持久的。只是在一个世纪后的现在，当电子媒介诸如摄影和录像从绘画中夺取了对先锋地位的控制后，塞尚的影响才开始渐渐减弱。

然而，费城艺术博物馆正在举办一个吸引人的展览会，它的目的在于证实毕加索、马蒂斯和其他14位继承塞尚风格的艺术家们的断言，这14人的艺术都形成于塞尚画作范例的影响。到五月中旬为止，塞尚继续显示着他的影响力。

"塞尚与穿越"将这位法国大师创作的大约60幅油画和水彩画与其他画家创造的大约120幅画同时展出：有欧洲画家诸如彼埃·蒙德里安、费尔南德·莱热、马克斯·贝克曼和阿尔伯特·贾赫梅蒂，美洲画家如马斯登·哈特利、查尔斯·德穆斯、贾斯泊·约翰斯和埃尔斯沃思·凯利。

展览的目的是阐释这些艺术风格的相似点，和表现塞尚怎样拓展了艺术家们的思考方式。面对这样的绘画题材，像在普罗旺斯地区塞尚家乡附近的《圣维克托瓦尔山》和他的重要静物画《苹果》，艺术家们不可能再简单地临摹自然，他们必须拆分解析它。立体派艺术家提供了这种变化的最鲜明的例子，但是 16 位当代艺术家，特别是凯利、布莱斯·马尔顿和加拿大摄影家杰夫·沃尔创造了更精湛的将塞尚的原理融入他们的作品中去的方法。

"塞尚与穿越"是出色而有影响的由过去 100 年间最有才华的画家们创作的现代派与后现代派艺术的作品集。它也是自 1996 年的回顾展（也是在费城，还有伦敦和巴黎）以来，塞尚的绘画在美国最令人难忘的纵览。蒙上述这位绘画大师的恩惠，这次是三个展览会合在一起举行。

单词注释

cubism ['kju:bizm] *n.* （美术）立体派

radical ['rædikəl] *adj.* 根本的，基本的

fade [feid] *v.* 凋谢，枯萎

vivid ['vivid] *adj.* 鲜艳的；鲜明的；强烈的

实用句型 & 词组

Strawberries disagree with me.（不适宜，有害）

He denied any role in the robbery.（作用，任务）

He wrote back to her out of courtesy.（殷勤，好意）

翻译行不行

塞尚对他下一代人的影响是最强烈的，此外也被证实是极为持久的。

_____

评论家和学者们也许对确定现代艺术的开创者意见不一，但是几乎没有人否认塞尚作为助产士一样的关键作用。

_____

展览的目的是阐释这些艺术风格的相似点，和表现塞尚怎样拓展了艺术家们的思考方式。

_____